GOOD THINKING

A SELF-IMPROVEMENT APPROACH TO GETTING YOUR MIND TO GO FROM "HUH?" TO "HMM" TO "AHA!"

GOOD THINKING

A SELF-IMPROVEMENT APPROACH TO GETTING YOUR MIND TO GO FROM "HUH?" TO "HMM" TO "AHA!"

Robert Eidelberg

To order additional copies of this book, contact:
Xlibris LLC
1-888-795-4274
www.Xlibris.com
Orders@Xlibris.com
137303

Contents

Chapter 1: **Thinking About Thinking** / what the key thinking skills are for success in your personal life and your professional life; how consciously thinking about the thinking you do (*not* sub-consciously—but intentionally and purposefully) is the start to becoming a more empowered and effective thinker; how talking out loud to yourself as a rational person, as well as writing things down in a personal journal, can help you with your thinking.. 15

Chapter 2: **Keeping an Open—Or At Least Less Narrow—Mind** / what it means for a person to have an open mind (that person should be you; that mind should be yours); why keeping your mind as wide open as possible is essential to the thinking that you do 29

Chapter 3: **Internalizing Several Desirable "Do's" and a Few Definite "Don'ts" of Good Thinking** / how "us" and "them" thinking can lead to stereotyped thinking (not a good thing!); how making unexamined assumptions can stop thinking before it starts; how internalizing certain mental "do's" and "don'ts" can improve your thinking.. 45

Chapter 4: **Thinking in Generalizations** / how generalizations work; why, generally speaking, it is essential to be able to think, speak, and write in generalizations; why it is important to examine the truth or falsity of our generalizations..................... 67

Chapter 5: **Thinking Through Categories** / why it is that you know more than you think you do; what categories are—and how you can use them to help you recall factual information and memorize (by rote!) new sets of facts; how thinking through categories enables you to order, organize, and process your thinking, your speaking, and your writing 85

Chapter 6: **Thinking Factually Through—and Beyond—Our So-Called Right Answers** / what it most likely means when you tell someone—or someone tells you—"that's right"; where the line is between "fact" and "opinion" and how "thin" that line can be; why "factually speaking" may simply be "a difference of opinion"; how to think more in terms of "probability" and "possibility" and less in terms of dogmatic "certainty"; how rote learning and teaching to the test are not in the spirit or service of good thinking 101

Chapter 7: **Thinking Factually Through—and Out From—Our So-Called Wrong Answers, Errors, Mistakes, and Failures** / what it means when your answer is "wrong" or "you are mistaken"; how you can learn from "the error of your ways"; what it means to think "definitionally"; how failure can be the foundation for success; how cause-and-effect thinking is anything but casual 115

Chapter 8: **Thinking Laterally (Outside the Box)** / how to "fix" your fixated assumptive thinking; how to think laterally (outside the box) and, possibly, more creatively; how to use brainstorming in the service of lateral thinking 125

Chapter 9: **Thinking Visually Through "Picture This!"** / "thinking pictorially" is one of several types of *non-verbal* thinking (thinking that bypasses the use of words) 143

Chapter 10: Thinking Metaphorically (Whenever You Have a Flight of Fancy) / how to understand what a metaphor "is" and what a metaphor "does"; in short, how to "nail" the concept of metaphor; how to appreciate what metaphors are for; how to be aware when and why you—and others—use metaphor after metaphor after metaphor like "a running faucet"; how to know when to put "the brakes" on your metaphors, especially if you are mixing the ones that you make; how to avoid ("like the plague!") metaphors that are clichés.................................... 145

Chapter 11: Thinking Wittily (A Walk on the Wilde Side) / why "wit" is even in a book about thinking; why they're wild about Wilde; how to channel Oscar Wilde................................ 167

Chapter 12: Thinking Symbolically (It's Way More Representative of Your Thinking Than You Think) / how, and when, and why a symbol "stands for" something else (when it is not sitting down on the job); how to knock the legs out from under a symbol that may still stand for something but has been standing for that same something for so long that the symbolism is little more than a crutch that, in effect, undermines good thinking.. 173

Chapter 13: Thinking Ironically (Or At Least "Interestingly") / what the three most commonly used kinds of irony are; why there is no "iron" in irony (how verbal irony differs from sarcasm); why irony is even considered to be "good thinking." 183

Chapter 14: Thinking It Through to the End Without Jumping to Conclusions / final thoughts: Huh? Hmm. Aha! For self-improvement, mind your mind.................................. 197

Dedication: "At least put the perishables away"

In appreciation of my mother, Esther, and her five
remarkable sisters, "the Binder Girls"—my loving
and thoughtful aunts: Faygee (who taught me how
to type for real), Minnie, Mary, Pearlie, and Bella
(who baby-sat me for years)

ABOUT THE AUTHOR

A former journalist, Robert Eidelberg served for nineteen and a half years as the chair of the English department of William Cullen Bryant High School in New York City and a total of 32 years as a secondary school English teacher in the New York City public school system.

Upon "graduating" from Bryant High School, Mr. Eidelberg was an educational and editorial consultant and author for Amsco School Publications and a writing instructor at Audrey Cohen Metropolitan College of New York as well as at Queensborough Community College of the City University of New York.

For the past 15 years, Mr. Eidelberg has been a college adjunct supervising undergraduate and graduate student teachers in secondary English education for both the State University of New York at New Paltz and the City University of New York, where he has specialized in teaching the culminating secondary English education practicum seminar at CUNY's Hunter College campus.

As a working author with a fondness for fictional characters and somewhat lengthy subtitles for his books, Mr. Eidelberg recently published a careers book on what it takes to become and remain an effective secondary school teacher and not burn out—**SO YOU THINK YOU MIGHT LIKE TO TEACH: 23 Fictional Teachers (for Real!) Model How to Become and Remain a Successful Teache**r.

He is currently completing a self-improvement "companion book" to **GOOD THINKING** called **PLAYING DETECTIVE: A Self-Improvement Approach to Becoming a More Mindful Thinker, Reader, and Writer By Solving Mysteries**.

Robert Eidelberg lives in the Park Slope neighborhood of Brooklyn, New York, with his life partner of 40 years and their 13-year-old part-hound, part-Doberman dog Marlowe, a very mindful mutt.

*"An idea that is not dangerous is unworthy
of being called an idea at all"*
—*Oscar Wilde*

1

Thinking About Thinking

Think About It

In this introductory chapter to **Good Thinking** you will discover:

- what the key thinking skills are for success in your personal life and your professional life,
- how consciously thinking about the thinking you do (*not* sub-consciously—but intentionally and purposefully) is the start to becoming a more empowered and effective thinker,
- how talking out loud to yourself as a rational person, as well as writing things down in a personal journal, can help you with your thinking.

Introduction to the Way This Book Works

But not quite yet.

First let's start with you.

Despite the fact that you're holding this book in your hands and reading these words—and now these words—you may at the same time be thinking that you don't need any book to tell you how to think (*how dare you, author of* **Good Thinking***, tell me how to think!*) or even to try to teach you how to do it any better than you're already doing it. Am I right? Or close?

Perhaps you're saying to yourself that thinking comes naturally, that you do it all the time, and that you don't need to think about it. It's a "no brainer."

Or, possibly, you may be feeling that thinking is hard work (you're absolutely right that it can be) and you would rather not question why you have this book in your hands. After all, although there *must* be a reason you're still reading these very words these many paragraphs into this book's first chapter, you're sure to find out soon enough from the author of **Good Thinking** what that reason is without too much effort on your part. (In that case, it's likely that you're also thinking: "Let somebody else do the hard work for me!")

No matter what you think you believe about the thinking that you do, "a mind," as popular wisdom frequently reminds us, "is a terrible thing to waste." So, and here comes the "answer" you may have been waiting for: the underlying philosophy of this book on mindful self-improvement is that "good thinking" is what you accomplish when you put your mind to it. Or, to put it another way, if you "mind your mind," you can, in fact, become the best possible thinker you can be.

The Purpose of This Book

The major purpose of **Good Thinking** (it's only reason for being, actually) is to help you improve your present ability as a thinker by giving you clarity in and practice with the key thinking attitudes and skills that produce good thinking—in human beings; so don't go trying this book at home on your dog.

These thinking attitudes and skills—presented, explained, exemplified, reviewed, and reinforced in **Good Thinking**'s fourteen relatively short chapters—will help you teach yourself over time, through structured practice, how to "get your mind to go from "Huh?" (or, perhaps "Duh?," if you feel your mind sometimes starts with that attitude) to "Hmm" and then on to "Aha!" **Good Thinking**'s subtitle seeks to tell it as it will be. Some of these good thinking attitudes and skills are:

- how to take notice of and pay attention to the thinking that you do and make it work for you in your life,
- how to have—and keep—an open mind,
- how to examine assumptions and avoid stereotypical thinking,
- how to respond to "right" and "wrong" answers, and, how, especially, to learn from your "not-so-good" thinking,
- how to recognize actual instances of "cause and effect" reasoning,
- how to distinguish opinion from fact both in your own thinking and in the thinking of others (who always think they know what they're talking about),
- how to generalize from specifics, details, and examples,
- how to categorize,
- how to reason "reasonably,"
- how to pay attention, notice, observe, analyze, make connections, synthesize, and see patterns,
- how to consider possible and probable conclusions (with some degree of certainty),
- how to watch out for fixated inside-the-box thinking and how to embrace thinking laterally (outside the box),

- how to think figuratively (metaphorically and symbolically), and
- how to think ironically (and I mean that seriously).

Good Thinking will give your mind on-going opportunities to ask itself a variety of thought-provoking questions in the service of thinking clearly, thinking critically, and thinking creatively. If some of these thinking skills are already a part of your thinking repertoire, you will see exactly how they have served you well in a school setting, or in your job or avocational work, or in your day-to-day life. Why will this become obvious? Because we live in a world that not only values good thinking but also demands it for personal and professional success.

How This Book Is Structured to Work for You

Each chapter of **Good Thinking** opens with a preview of the thinking skills and attitudes you will work to master in that chapter; you will find this preview under the heading **Think About It**. Next comes four sections: **Mind Set**, **What Do You Think?**, **Reflections**, and **Assessing Your Thinking**. Here's how these chapter sections compare and contrast with and complement one another:

Mind Set

A person has a "mind set" when he or she responds to or interprets a particular situation in a familiar, predictable, or, you might even say, pre-determined way. This "way" reflects the fact that this person has a fixed mental attitude—call it a "default setting," if you like, on a subject. In this book, "Mind Set" sections serve as a mental set-up—an alert or prompt—for a situation you will be asked to *do* something about.

What Do You Think?

Taking you step by step through your own thought processes, "What Do You Think?" sections ask you to do very specific kinds of thinking about particular "Mind Set" situations; they are presented either in the form of a series of questions, a problem, or an activity. There are often multiple "What Do You Think?" sections even in the briefest of chapters.

Reflections

Reflecting on something involves giving it extended thought and careful consideration. The "Reflections" sections in each chapter of **Good Thinking** demonstrate the human mind at work and at play (that human mind happens to be mine); these "Reflections" sections serve—I hope!—both as models of good thinking and as one of the book's major means to further good thinking on the part of the reader.

Assessing Your Thinking

These sections of **Good Thinking** appear throughout each chapter after most "Reflections" sections and give you, the reader who is taking this "self-improvement approach," an opportunity to assess, or test, your learning of the various thinking skills and attitudes featured in that chapter.

Here is your first experience (a preview, a tryout, a template) with this book's interactive sections (the four just described); they are usually found multiple times in each and every chapter.

Mind Set

The Human Mind

Many human languages—and this shouldn't surprise you—contain sayings that have something to do with the human mind. Here are two of them from the English language, one of which you saw earlier in this introductory chapter: (1) "A mind is a terrible thing to waste"; (2) "A person's mind *is* the person."

What Do You Think?

Create a third possible saying combining the words and ideas of the two sayings presented in the above "Mind Set."

Reflections

Thinking About Thinking (Who Knew?)

The process you have just gone through—examining how your own mind went about the task of producing a third saying—is called "thinking about thinking."

How do *you* do your own thinking about thinking? (And don't say that you never have done any such thing! It's just not true; it's just not human.) Think about that—how *you* do your own thinking about thinking—for *at least a little bit* before you read any further. (The mindful self-improvement work of this book begins now!)

Okay. Did you come up with something like the following as expressed in the words of someone who was asked the same question you were? That person said: "I go back into my mind with a new and very different purpose, namely, to take a look at and put into words what my mind was *doing* when it was busy thinking about how to create a third saying made up of the ideas and words of the two sayings I was given."

Here is how that same person described, step by step, the mental process at work when asked to create a new saying from the two provided in the mental set-up or "mind set."

- *if* it is really *true* that a person's mind is a terrible thing to waste,
- *and* it is *also* really *true* that a person's mind *is* the person,
- *then*, it seems to me to *follow* (it seems logical, it appears reasonable to me) that a person is a terrible thing to waste *because* you can now *substitute* "person" for "person's mind" in the first saying since those two wordings now name or identify the same thing. This kind of reasoning makes sense to me because it's like, in basic arithmetic, saying $2 + 3 = 4 + 1$. "A person is a terrible thing to waste" is like saying 5 can be expressed as $2 + 3$ or $4 + 1$.

What Do You Think?

You may not be all that accustomed to doing much thinking about your own thinking. And you may not be all that comfortable with it. Not to worry. This book and you have just begun to work together. But since we have started, try to put into words, as that other person did, the thinking you did when you thought about how to create a third saying.

Then, compare and contrast ("comparing" and "contrasting" are ways of doing some very good thinking by talking about the noticeable similarities and differences between things); compare and contrast how you expressed your thinking about thinking and how that other person expressed his or her thinking.

Assessing Your Thinking

How Do You Feel?

What made you comfortable and what made you uncomfortable about going back and looking at and thinking about the thinking you did when you created your third saying?

Assessing Your Thinking

"Crazy" People Walking Around Talking to Themselves

A number of years ago, the comedian and comic writer Lily Tomlin joked about how the presence, then, of visibly "crazy" people walking around New York City talking out loud to themselves might be keeping prospective tourists from visiting the city. To help New York City with the question of lost tourist income, Ms. Tomlin considered (gave some thought to) this financial problem and came up with this possible solution: pair off the "crazy" people so that it would look as if they were talking not to themselves but to each other.

Ms. Tomlin's reasoning was based on the "mind set" fact that sane people (like you) often talk to themselves—either out loud or silently. These "talks" are really you having a conversation with yourself about your thinking; you are thinking about your thinking. So . . . . (Try putting into words the rest of the reasoning that leads to the "pairing off" solution.)

By the way, this "joke," as we said at the start, goes back "a number of years ago." Can you think of something that has been invented and widely marketed since then that might lead you to suggest another possible solution to the problem Ms. Tomlin worked on—a solution not involving any pairing of people. (Don't read any further until you've given yourself time to reflect.)

Did you come up with something like giving each "crazy" person a cellphone? Think about your thinking and tell how you came up with that solution, a solution that creates the appearance of sane behavior on New York City's streets. If you came up with another possible solution to the problem, think about your thinking so that you can tell someone how you came up with that solution. Then, try writing down your thinking in a personal journal so that you can reflect back on it at another time because you now have it "on record" to, literally, "re-view," view again. (Writing things down physicalizes memory, makes memory tangible, retrievable; writing is all about "wrote" memory—not "rote" memory.)

Mind Set

Some Practice Thinking About Five Different Kinds of Thinking
Let's try some more "thinking about thinking," this time with the actual word "think" and how its meaning changes (which it does) when we place a short word after it—short words like *about, of, over, up, through.*

What Do You Think?

Think about how the nature of your thinking changes when each of these fairly short italicized words is included as part of your thinking process: what is different about the kind of thinking you are doing when you do each of the following five types? Put the difference into words—and either say the words aloud or write them down, since writing things down actually helps you not only with your memory but also with your thinking. (It is easier to re-visit a thought that's right there in front of you on a piece of paper than to go blindly searching for it in the folds of your brain.)

    (a) to think about something,
    (b) to think of something,
    (c) to think over something (to think something over),
    (d) to think up something (to think something up),
    (e) to think something through (to think through something).

Now, take another last look at these five "thinks" and either write down or say aloud which of them you think you were doing when you thought about what was different about each of the five.

Reflections

It's Just a Thought, But What *Is* a Thought?

Here's a thought: let's think for a moment about "thought."

A story is told about how, at the start of the current century, a husband and wife pledged several hundred million dollars over a period of twenty years to the Massachusetts Institute of Technology to finance research on the workings of the brain.

At the announcement of the donation, the wife said that she traced her interest in the brain to when she was five years old and visited a science museum. Her parents showed her a brain in formaldehyde, and she asked them, "Can you touch thought? Does it have a physical presence?" Then she added at the time of the donation, "And so maybe we can figure that out."

As a young child, this woman had wondered out loud about something that many of us might never have given a thought to. Her mind asked herself a question: "Just what is a thought?" And then she re-phrased the question as she turned to her parents and asked, "Can you touch thought? Does it have a physical presence?"

One of the great things about thinking well (practicing good thinking) is that one question can lead to another and another, even though none of them may immediately get to "the answer." According to a Chinese proverb, "a journey of a thousand miles begins with one step." Using the same "good thinking" from earlier in this chapter, if we agree that a question is (or is like) a step along the road to an answer, then we can say that "a journey of a thousand miles to an answer begins with just one single question."

One of the things we do with questions in the English language is we "raise" them when we want to know about something we are puzzled by or want to know more about. "Raising a question," if we visualize those words, is an "up" thing to do—and we often emphasize that "up-ness" by putting our hand into the air.

Assessing Your Thinking

One Question Can Lead to Another

Do you agree with the American writer James Thurber when he says that "it is better to know some of the questions than all of the answers"? Can you put into words why you agree or disagree or agree and disagree? Think about it. And then think about what comes next as we come to the end of Chapter 1.

What Do You Think?

Does "thought" have a physical presence for you? Can you touch it? What *is* a "thought"? What does it mean to be "thoughtful"?

Mind Set

Being Thoughtful

Usually when we say that someone has been "thoughtful," we mean that the person acted in a "caring" and "concerned" way. Literally, we are saying that the person has taken the time and made the mental effort to be "full of thought" before he or she took action. Since speaking is a quite articulate form of action (an aside: you might want to think about whether you subscribe to the belief, always, that "Actions speak louder than words"), we can agree that thoughtful people think before they say something that might be incorrect, or inappropriate, or hurtful.

What Do You Think?

What does it mean to say that a person is "thoughtless"? How might that meaning connect with the idea that the person has not given something any thought?

Assessing Your Thinking

Thoughtlessness

Thoughtlessness, in all of its meanings, is not a good thing. The potential of the human mind for thinking is vast, and "good thinking" is what you accomplish when you put your mind to it. To be the best possible thinker you can be takes work and practice in thinking clearly, thinking constructively, thinking critically, and thinking creatively. Consciously thinking about the thinking you do during your day and throughout your life is the foundation for becoming a more effective and empowered thinker in your personal and professional life.

Think about it. Put your thoughts into words that you then say aloud or write down—before you go on to Chapter 2.

Assessing Your Thinking

A Famous Anecdote (Perhaps Apocryphal, or Too, Too Good to Be True)

The story is told of the American writer Gertrude Stein as she lay on her deathbed: her lifelong friend and companion, Alice B. Toklas, leaned close to Ms. Stein's face and asked, "Gertrude, what is the answer?"

Ms. Stein replied, "What is the question?" And then Gertrude Stein died.

In a personal journal that you might want to keep about the thinking you do, comment on this very well-known anecdotal moment.

- what question—in your own words—do you think Alice B. Toklas was asking?
- what question—in your own words—do you think Gertrude Stein was asking?
- think about the thinking you did to respond to these two questions and then include in your journal a description of that thinking,

- at some future point in time, read out loud to someone what you have written in your journal (someone you care to share your journal entry with); after thoughtfully listening to and thoughtfully responding to that person's out loud thinking about your recorded thinking, go back to your journal and think, in writing, again,
- a deathbed bonus: the story is told (but it may be apocryphal) that the Irish playwright and wit Oscar Wilde made the following critical comment as he looked around the unfamiliar room his dying body was lying in: "Either that wallpaper has to go or I will"; if you find Wilde's remark to be "witty," try explaining why you do and, since Wilde knew he was close to death, where is the seriousness usually associated with the subject of death located in Wilde's words?
- compare and contrast Wilde's deathbed comment with Gertrude Stein's.

2

Keeping an Open Mind

Think About It

In this chapter you will discover:

- what it means for a person to have an open mind (that person should be you; that mind should be yours),
- why keeping your mind as wide open as possible is essential to the thinking that you do.

Mind Set

A Conversation from a Television Play

You are about to read a brief conversation that takes place in a jury room at the conclusion of a criminal trial. The two jurors are characters in the 1954 teleplay "Twelve Angry Men," written by the American playwright Reginald Rose and later expanded by him into both a stage and a film version.

Although "Twelve Angry Men" is a work of fiction, Rose based it on an actual experience he had while serving as a juror on a murder case trial in New York City. As a writer of literature, Rose took the facts of the case and worked them through his imagination to create the play "Twelve Angry Men."

As the play opens, the trial of a 19-year-old boy accused of murder is just concluding. In fact, the opening lines of "Twelve Angry Men" consist of the presiding judge's instructions to the twelve jurors. He tells the all-male jury that the law requires an unanimous agreement on a verdict—and it requires the death penalty if that 12 to 0 verdict is "guilty as charged."

The jurors retire to the jury room and soon agree to take an open vote to get a sense of the group's feelings about the case. Eleven jurors raise their hand for "guilty"; one juror raises his for "not guilty."

The conversation that follows is between the one juror who has voted not guilty (Juror B we'll call him) and one of the other eleven jurors (our Juror A). The style of language of the conversation (as well as that of the entire play) reflects the 1950's New York City setting of the play and the diverse socio-economic backgrounds of the twelve jurors. Knowing what you know from Chapter 1 about the importance of consciously thinking about the thinking we all do, consider how "good" the thinking is of Jurors A and B.

> **Juror A:** He's guilty for sure. There's not a doubt in the whole world. We shoulda been done already . . . . You think he's not guilty?
>
> **Juror B:** I don't know. It's possible.

Juror A: I don't know you, but I'm bettin' you've never been wronger in your life. Y'oughta wrap it up. You're wastin' your time.

Juror B: Supposing you were the one on trial?

Juror A: I'm not used to supposing. I'm just a working man. My boss does the supposing. But I'll try one. Supposing you talk us all outa this, and the kid really did knife . . . (the victim)?

What Do You Think?

In your opinion, how good a thinker is Juror B? What exactly do you base your opinion on? What do you think of the question he raises for Juror A—and why do you think that? (Feel free to express yourself in your personal journal.)

Reflections

Thinking About Juror A's Thinking

Although Juror A says he's "not used to supposing," he goes ahead and does some "supposing," raising a question of his own for Juror B to answer. In addition, Juror A takes the time to do some thinking about his own thinking ("I'm not used to supposing. I'm just a working man. My boss does the supposing"). How might this have come about? Before you read on, think about that for a bit and try to suggest an explanation or reason that you feel is at least "possible" or, better still, might even be "probable" (actually likely but not certain).

Here's one possible "reason-able" explanation: in asking Juror A "Supposing you were the one on trial?" Juror B wants Juror

A to put himself in the nineteen-year-old defendant's place. Basically he is asking Juror A, "Wouldn't *you* want a jury to take a reasonable (within reason) amount of time deciding *your* fate?" Juror B apparently *assumes* (takes for granted without giving the matter any real thought) that everyone would answer "yes" to that question.

However, Juror A does not immediately or automatically answer with a "yes"; instead, Juror A reacts and responds to the "supposing" part of Juror B's question, interpreting the situation Juror B has purposely put him in as a personal challenge. Rising to the perceived challenge, Juror A first does some thinking about the kind of thinking person he is ("I'm not used to supposing. I'm just a working man. My boss does the supposing") and then retaliates with a challenging question of his own for Juror B to grapple with: "Supposing you talk us all outa this, and the kid really did knife . . . (the victim)?"

The way Juror A sees it, he's a worker—and the job of a worker is, by definition, to work. And what does he see his boss's job to be (since his boss is not a worker but the boss)? The job of a boss is, again by definition, to boss. And to Juror A, "bossing" is not, definitionally, "working"; bossing is for Juror A, at least in part, about doing all the thinking required in the work environment. And, to think this through to a logical conclusion, it therefore follows for Juror A that any thinking by a boss is not a form of "working."

Trying to do the same kind of reasoning we used in Chapter 1, Juror A has concluded, in short, that since the job of a worker is to work and the job of a boss is to think (and we are what we do; we are our jobs), then, logically, no worker can be also a thinker because thinking belongs exclusively to the identity called "boss."

What Juror A has excluded from his "not-so-good" thinking is the possibility that certain (or even all) kinds of work done by non-bosses (including Juror A's work!) require some kind of thinking. This probable fact simply does not occur to Juror A (he doesn't give it a thought). Why is that?

Perhaps it's because Juror A *believes* (incorrectly, as it turns out since it's a fact that he thinks) that anyone who is "just a working man" is not only "not used to supposing" but also that all the "supposing" on a job is always done by the boss of the job. (When people *believe* something, they "take it on faith"; they do not examine it—think much about it—in order to prove it to be correct. Thought and belief are not the same thing; if anything, beliefs are more similar to feelings or instincts.)

It's instructive, too, that Juror A *may* have decided at some point in his life that being "a working man" is not as worthy an activity as being a "supposing" man (a boss). This possible conclusion is based on contrasting the different meanings of "I'm a working man" with what Juror A actually says by way of identifying himself: "I'm just a working man." "Just" is a small word, but it carries a big weight of meaning.

And yet, Juror A decides to break out of the less valued role he sees himself in and to do a bit of "supposing," after all. Perhaps he would explain his action as the "exception that proves the rule" of his way of life, since "not *used* to supposing" suggests that Juror A may do some supposing after all—but only on rare occasions like this one.

What Do You Think?

What do you think of the question Juror A raises for Juror B—and why do you think the way you do? In your opinion, how good a thinker is Juror A—and what do you base your opinion on?

Reflections

Having an Open Mind

People who have an open mind are willing to listen to the ideas, opinions, and explanations of others who may or may not share the same beliefs or think the same way they do. Unlike people who are narrow-minded or close-minded (can you picture in your mind what those kinds of minds look like?), open-minded people (now visualize *that*) are receptive to different possibilities, additional facts, new developments, and changing circumstances.

Open-minded individuals have not *solidified* their thinking on a matter once and for all; they're more *fluid*. Instead of seeing a request to "think again" as a challenge to their *certainty* about something and as a veiled threat to their intelligence, truly open-minded people see "thinking again" as an opportunity—not as a problem.

Assessing Your Thinking

Can You Open Your Mind a Bit Wider?

In your personal journal, tell who you think has the more open mind—Juror A or Juror B—and give as many reasons as you can as to why you think so.

Mind Set

Other Jurors from "Twelve Angry Men" (and Their Dialogue)

As the play "Twelve Angry Men" progresses, testimony from the trial is re-examined in the jury room as the increasingly "angry men" try to change one another's minds and produce a unanimous verdict. If the twelve jurors (identified in the play as Jurors 1 through 12) cannot reach complete agreement (12 to 0) that the defendant is either guilty or not guilty, the judge will have to declare what is known as a "hung jury." In such cases, the jurors are dismissed from service and a new trial is set with twelve new jurors.

Coming up following this Mind Set are some additional lines of dialogue (and some action) from Reginald Rose's play involving most of the twelve now-angry jurors. (It's important to remember that the speaking style of the jurors reflects both the play's 1950's New York City setting and the different backgrounds of the individual men.)

As you read over their dialogue, do not be surprised to find yourself beginning to make some judgments about these jurors and the degree to which they have an open mind. (Good readers are always thinking and feeling as they go about their reading.)

What Do You Think?

A Role-Playing Prompt for You

To help you focus your reading, here's a prompt: pretend that you are the nineteen-year-old boy on trial for his life. In some mysterious way, you are able to eavesdrop on the discussion going on in the juryroom. Your life is in these men's hands. Who are you glad is on the jury? Who do you wish was not? Why is that?

Juror 1: Maybe if the gentleman who's disagreeing (Juror 8, the juror who voted not guilty that we have referred to as Juror B up to now) . . . can tell us why. You know, tell us what he thinks, we could show him where he's probably mixed up.

Juror 8 (responding): I sat there in court for six days listening while the evidence built up. You know everybody sounded so positive that I started to get a peculiar feeling about this trial. I mean, nothing is *that* positive. I had questions I would have liked to ask. Maybe they wouldn't have meant anything. I don't know.

Juror 2: Well, it's hard to put into words. I just . . . think he's guilty. I thought it was obvious from the word go.

Juror 3 (speaking to Juror 8): Well, look, do you really think he's innocent?

Juror 8 (responding to Juror 3): I don't know.

Juror 8 (later in the play): I don't know whether I believe it (the defendant's story) or not. Maybe I don't.

Juror 3: I really think this is one of those open and shut cases.

Juror 3 (later in the play): I really think the guy's guilty. You couldn't change my mind if you talked for a hundred years.

Juror 10: Now you're not going to tell us that we're supposed to believe that kid, knowing what he is. Listen, I've lived among 'em all my life. You can't believe a word they say. You know that. I mean, they're born liars.

Juror 9 (speaking directly to Juror 10): Do you think you were born with a monopoly on the truth?

Juror 4: I don't see any need for arguing like this. I think we ought to be able to behave like gentlemen.

Juror 4 (later in the play): If we're going to discuss this case, let's discuss the facts.

Juror 11: I don't believe I must be loyal to one side or the other. I'm simply asking questions.

Juror 7 (walks away from Juror 9 while Juror 9 is in the midst of talking with him about the case)

Juror 8 (speaking to Juror 9 about Juror 7's walking away from him): He can't hear you. He never will.

Juror 9 (changing his vote from "guilty" to "not guilty"): The boy on trial is probably guilty. But I want to hear more. Right now the vote is ten to two.

What Do You Think?

In your journal, write an entry from the point of view of the nineteen-year-old boy. Be as creative as you like as long as you do not change or distort the reality of what the eavesdropping defendant overheard (the above lines of dialogue in the Mind Set).

As the boy, react to and reflect on what the jurors said and did. When you have completed your journal entry, use what you have written to think about the following questions:

- which of these jurors are you happy are on the jury deciding your fate? Why? Where have any of these jurors shown themselves to have an open mind?
- you should be able to predict the next question: which of these jurors are you sorry are on the jury? Why? Where have any of these jurors shown themselves to be either narrow-minded or close-minded?
- which of these jurors are you undecided about or have mixed feelings about? (Did you see this question coming? If you did, tell yourself how you were able to see it coming.)

Reflections

Having and Keeping an Open Mind

Felix Frankfurter, a renowned American Supreme Court justice, once said that "Wisdom too often never comes, and so one ought not to reject it merely because it comes late."

How is Justice Frankfurter's remark an example of having an open mind or being broad-minded (the opposite of narrow-minded)?

The job of the nine members of the Supreme Court of the United States is to examine the American Constitution and the country's laws whenever a controversial issue comes before them for a thoughtful decision based on expert research and clear understanding. In his quoted comment, Justice Frankfurter—with all his education, experience, and intellectual capability—admits that true wisdom is frequently beyond mankind's mental grasp and the acceptance of this fact, he suggests, should humble us all and keep us from thinking too highly of ourselves.

All of us, Justice Frankfurter advises, should have and keep an open mind; we should always be receptive to new and different ideas since true wisdom, when it comes at all, may come only many years after we have formed our first opinion on a particular matter based on the facts available to us at the time. Just as "first impressions" may be succeeded by later ones (sometimes based on the "second opinions" of others), all "certainties" should be considered tentative, temporary, subject to change (with or without notice); one thing is certain: the possibility always exists that new evidence, later developments, and altered circumstances will arise to prompt us to change our minds.

The good thinker, Justice Frankfurter believes, welcomes wisdom whenever it comes knocking at the unlocked door of our minds; after all, human beings can and do make mistakes even when we do the very best we can with what we have. Good thinkers try to learn from their mistakes as they go about correcting their errors and altering their behavior. (More about this kind of good thinking in a later chapter.) When it comes to wisdom (and most people come to actual "wisdom" infrequently), late is better than never—and it is never too late to learn.

Mind Set

In Conclusion

An essential aspect of good thinking is the ability to have and keep an open mind. First impressions are just that—and "snap" judgments can be both dismissive and indicative of a mind that has snapped closed for good.

Keeping an open mind, however, takes vigilance, and patience, and practice. Sometimes, the people who are the first ones to open their mouths are also the first ones to close their minds. Keeping an open mind leaves room in the mansion of your mind for doubt. Keeping an open mind is an open invitation to re-visit and revise.

Assessing Your Thinking

An Original Scripted Dialogue

Select one of the jurors in the play "Twelve Angry Men" from those you decided are close-minded and create a conversation between him and a new character that represents *you*. (The British writer Henry Fielding defined "conversation" as the "reciprocal interchange of ideas, by which truth is examined (and) things are, in a manner, turned around, and sifted.")

Your purpose in this conversation is to get your chosen close-minded juror to open his mind up at least a little bit (and perhaps even more than that) to ideas presented to him in a scripted dialogue that you will write. To get the conversation started and to keep it going in the direction of achieving this purpose, you will need to create a series of original lines of dialogue for the character that represents you (since you are both invisible and voiceless in the actual play).

In writing the opening lines of dialogue for the close-minded juror, begin by making use of any of his words that you have from "Twelve Angry Men." Then, expand on these words and the ideas they represent in any way that you think your close-minded juror would if he were to continue to stick to his opinions while the character that represents you went about trying to convince him to open his mind to other possibilities. Finally, begin to change your juror's dialogue as he starts to show signs of being affected by the additional dialogue you are creating for the character that represents you.

If you can, find someone to act out this playlet with you, rehearsing it between the two of you at least once. Also, if you can pull another person or two in to function as the audience for your playlet, be sure to get some feedback from that audience after it has given you its polite round of applause.

Reflections

Thinking Through the Persuasive Essay—An Oral Argument

Not to scare you too much too soon, but this may be just the place in this book to introduce (or re-introduce) you to a kind of writing considerably more formal than the fairly informal personal journal—the persuasive essay. As its name suggests, the persuasive essay is a piece of writing whose *purpose* is to convince a potential reader (not you) that something that the writer (that *is* you) *believes* to be true is, in fact, true.

Since most people, quite rightly, will not adopt another person's point of view without being *made* to "see the light," persuasive essays need to do just that—persuade. Persuasive essays (which can also take the form of "oral arguments") are only as good as their facts and their reasoning (their solid reasons) for the purpose of getting someone to believe something that he or she does not currently believe (or believes the opposite of).

Writers of persuasive essays (and debaters in speeches) who fail at "good thinking" usually fail because they do little more than *tell* the other person to "Agree with me because I'm right (and you're wrong)" or insist that you "Take my word for it because I know what I'm talking about" (and thereby imply that you don't!) or beg that you "Believe me because I have all the facts." These are a waste of words; they are not even "friendly persuasion."

And because these non-convincing "essays" contain no actual points of persuasion, they do little more than ask, or beg, or require their readers to accept without question the writer's "authority." And why would anyone do that who has gone to the bother of paying attention? Good thinkers who are readers of persuasive essays (or listeners to oral arguments) expect and require substantial reasons and sufficient facts supporting those reasons before they can come to understand, and perhaps come around to, another person's point of view. A claimed victory is still debatable if it hasn't been clinched.

So, writers of persuasive essays must both *tell* what they believe in and *show* why others should change their minds and come over to their side of the issue. It is only a slight exaggeration to say that persuasive essays should sound like the kinds of closing arguments made in a court of law between lawyers for opposing sides. Persuasive essays, if they are about anything—and they are!—are about the weight of evidence for the case being made. Persuasion should never involve twelve—or any other number of—angry men or women; persuasion should invite rational people to try to come to an understanding.

Assessing Your Thinking

Thinking Through the Persuasive Essay

So, without getting too anxious about it, pick one of the following quotations to use in a short persuasive essay in which you try to persuade your potential reader that the judge in your quotation is a good example of a person who has kept an open mind. (If you would like, first, to see what such a short opinion piece of persuasion looks and sounds like, check out the better-argued letters to the editor of your daily newspaper; for longer pieces, see that newspaper's editorials, usually on the same page as its letters or on a nearby page, or read a few of that newspaper's columnists and commentators on its "op-ed" page, the page "opposite-the-editorial" page.)

- "the matter does not appear to me now as it appears to have appeared to me then." (Baron Bramwell, a British judge, in 1872),
- if there are other ways of gracefully and good-naturedly surrendering former views to a better considered position, I invoke them all." (Robert H. Jackson, an American Supreme Court justice, in 1950),
- "I hope it is enlightenment on my part, and acceptable even if a little late." (David H. Souter, an American Supreme Court justice, in 2000).

3

Internalizing Several Desirable "Do's" and a Few Definite "Don'ts" of Good Thinking

Think About It

In this chapter you will discover:

- how "us" and "them" thinking can lead to stereotyped thinking (not a good thing!),
- how making unexamined assumptions can stop thinking before it starts,
- how internalizing certain mental "do's" and "don'ts" can improve your thinking.

Mind Set

In the Spotlight: Juror 10 from "Twelve Angry Men"

Remember Juror 10 from the play "Twelve Angry Men"? He's one of the more memorable ones, the one who says, "Now you're not going to tell us that we're supposed to believe that kid, knowing what he is. Listen, I've lived among 'em all my life. You can't believe a word they say. You know that. I mean, they're born liars."

What Do You Think?

Count the number of times Juror 10 makes use of "I"/"my," "we"/"us" references, as well as the number of times he uses "he" and "they"/"them." What possible conclusions can you make about the mind set Juror 10 has? Based on your life's experiences, when people talk about "them," are the feelings associated with their words positive or negative?

Reflections

"Us" and "Them" Thinking

If Juror 10's thinking were to be represented by circles, not only would the two circles not intersect, they would probably be located quite a distance from each other. "Us" and "Them" thinking can be seen as looking like this:

$$\left(\text{US} \right) \qquad\qquad \left(\text{THEM} \right)$$

Distant, non-over-lapping circles could also be used to represent the two groups of teenagers in the American composer Leonard Bernstein's 1950's musical drama "West Side Story" (inspired by William Shakespeare's 16th-century dramatic tragedy "Romeo and Juliet").

In "Romeo and Juliet," the aristocratic parents of Romeo Montague and Juliet Capulet have been feuding for years. Then, one day, their respective children, the title characters Romeo and Juliet, meet and fall madly in love. In this classic ill-fated love story, the two young lovers assume (take for granted without examining sufficient evidence) that if their parents found out, they would probably not let their teenage children continue to see each other and, equally unlikely, one day give their blessing for them to get married. (In both classic Greek and Shakespearean drama, weddings at the end of a play take place only in comedies.) As a direct result of their probably correct assumption, Romeo and Juliet decide to keep their love a secret from their feuding families—and the consequences of that decision are tragic.

A similar assumption is at work in Leonard Bernstein's 20th-century classic musicalization of Shakespeare's tragedy. However, in "West Side Story," the foundational feud is not between two noble families but between two turf-warring ethnic street gangs on the west side of the borough of Manhattan in New York City—Polish Americans and Latino Americans. In this modern-day version of Shakespeare's tragedy of young love, the lives of Maria, a first-generation Latina American, and Tony, a second-generation Polish American, have intersected because they have fallen in love across ethnic group divisions.

If that wasn't complicated enough (and it is!), Maria's best friend, Anita, holds Tony responsible for the gang war death of *her* boyfriend who, to make matters worse, was Maria's brother. In a powerful song about these complications late in the musical, Anita tells Maria:

> A boy like that, who'll kill your brother, forget that boy
> and find another—one of your own kind, stick to your
> own kind.

Anita's song is revealing: "one of your own kind" is "us" and "a boy like that" is "them." (Interesting side note: when Leonard

Bernstein first started work on his musicalization of "Romeo and Juliet," its working title was "East Side Story" because the original Catholic and Jewish religious groups of the story historically fought over turf on the lower East side of Manhattan.)

So, let's look one more time at the equally revealing "us" and "them" mentality behind Juror 10's words quoted in the Mind Set at the start of this chapter. There's "us," the good guys, and there's "them," the bad guys—and that's all there is to it.

The bad guys are all liars (not any of "us" are liars, because we're the good guys). Even better (actually, worse), the bad guys are *born* bad, so of course lying comes *naturally* to them; that's just the way they *are*; *everybody knows* this to be a *fact* and, oh, yes, "that kid," you can see, is one of them; so there's nothing more to say.

Mind Set

Stereotyping and Prejudice

"Us" and "them" thinking is often the basis for the kind of far-from-good thinking known as stereotyping, which dictionaries define as a "mind set" that creates an image of someone or something that is oversimplified, formulaic, and unvarying. When individuals think in stereotypes and thus view the world through the lens of a camera with a single setting that sees only "group" shots, they wind up with an automatically selected filter that covers over what they are actually trying to clearly frame and focus in on.

Instead of discovering what's actually out there to be immediately and specifically experienced, individuals who think in stereotypes wind up distorting their day-to-day experiences through an unreal stereotype functioning as their view-finder. For these individuals, any *single or particular* "he or she"/"him or her" or "it" is always experienced as a *group* "them." And, more often than not, "them" has for these individuals a built-in association that is negative. Although people who think in stereotypes can be, and are, guilty of stereotypes that cast the "them" in an unreal or unrealistic positive light, the ugliest stereotypes encountered are the negative ones. Whichever, negative or positive, when you hear people talking about those stereotypical "them," your thinking antenna should shoot right up.

Individuals like Juror 10 always have this controlling picture in their minds of an entire class or group of people that keeps them from actually looking at and truly seeing a person from that group as an individual who deserves to be experienced immediately and directly, without any preconceived notions. Juror 10 is the kind of thinker who, though he doesn't actually say it, believes that "If you've seen one, you've seen them all." Thinking stereotypically, Juror 10 sees the boy in the murder case as a "what he is," not as a "who he is" when he says, "That kid, knowing what he is."

It should come as no surprise to you as you think about this that stereotyping goes hand in hand with prejudice. The prefix "pre" in "prejudice" means "before," and the root or stem of the word "prejudice"—"jud"—means what it means in "judgment." The word "prejudice" literally means a judgment formed beforehand, without actual knowledge or examination of the facts before one's eyes.

What Do You Think?

Find and comment on other examples of prejudice in the rest of Juror 10's dialogue.

Mind Set

Stereotyping and Assumption-Making

Individuals who make assumptions take something for granted or accept something as true without sufficiently examining evidence or proof (the very essence of good persuasive essay writing, you will recall). Such people, in effect, start with a conclusion rather than come to one. They don't even have to "jump to a conclusion"(which good thinkers would never do, anyway); they're already there at the get-go.

What they have done, if you are familiar with how the board game Monopoly is played, is they have "passed GO and collected $200" even *before* the Monopoly board has been opened for play, never making the trip around the four sides of the game board; that would be active, real playing or, in this comparison, actual thinking. And, to complete this extended comparison, Monopoly's consequence of "landing in jail" would, for these "players," be the equivalent, in the real world, of both personal and social embarrassment—and, perhaps, *one would hope*, backtracking, recanting, apologizing, and even rethinking the problematic nature of thinking stereotypically.

Reflections

Juror 10's Assumptions

When Juror 10 states so confidently to the other jurors that "you know that," he is also guilty of making the assumption that they all share his prejudice against the ethnic group to which the nineteen-year-old boy belongs and so would—of course!—agree that "they" are all natural-born liars. Yet, if Juror 10 had given the matter at least a little bit of thought, he might have quickly realized that there was a good statistical chance in a jury chosen from the residents of an obviously quite diverse city like New York that at least one of the other eleven jurors would not be so narrow-minded or close-minded as he was when it came, at least, to ethnic groups. New Yorkers come in two forms: those who are born there and those who move there because if you are at all different, you fit right in.

What Do You Think?

- where else has Juror 10 been guilty of *assumptive thinking* (what other assumptions has Juror 10 made)?
- juror 10's dialogue is alive with words and phrases that show "being prejudiced against" in action; can you think of some examples of individuals who are prejudiced "in favor of" someone or something that belongs to a stereotyped group?
- suppose (assume the role of a "supposing" type person), that Juror 10 told you emphatically that he is not a prejudiced person. "I am," he might argue, "a man of strong convictions, a true believer. I think the way I do based on years of experience; in fact, I've lived among 'em all my life." As a good thinker, how would you answer Juror 10 to counter his argument?
- can someone who is prejudiced be a good thinker? Give the thinking behind your response,
- can someone who thinks in stereotypes be a good thinker? Give the thinking behind your response.

Mind Set

Selected Dialogue of the Three Characters in the Short Story "After You, My Dear Alphonse"

The 1943 short story "After You, My Dear Alphonse" by the American writer Shirley Jackson shows us three individuals: a young boy by the name of Johnny Wilson, the boy's mother, and Johnny's friend Boyd. Not shown to the reader but referred to by the characters are Boyd's mother and father, Boyd's sister, and, most significant of all, the group of people Mrs. Wilson sees when she looks at Boyd but sees not "a who" but "a what"—a stereotype.

What Do You Think?

Although "After You, My Dear Alphonse" is a very short story, it speaks volumes on the long history of stereotypical thinking about the subject of race in American life. By all means, locate and read this heavily dialogued short story on your own at any point in your involvement with this chapter of **Good Thinking**, but, right now, direct your attention to the per character sequenced dialogue quoted below as a way of considering how people *are* the words they choose to say, *are* the tone of voice in which they say what they say, *are* their facial expressions and their body language while they are saying what they say, and *are* what they purposely keep themselves from saying (except in the privacy of their own minds).

More particularly, check out these sequenced excerpts of dialogue within each character for instances of prejudice and stereotyping and for examples of unexamined assumptions on the part of the story's three characters: Mrs. Wilson; her young son Johnny

Wilson; and Johnny's friend Boyd. (Don't look for "Alphonse," by the way; "Alphonse" is a man's given name that was fairly common in Great Britain in the nineteenth century but not so much anymore; the story's title is actually quoting an old-time expression of manners that means giving first preference for entering a room, for example, to another person: "I will enter the room only after you do, my dear Alphonse; you get to go first as a sign of my good upbringing."

Sequenced dialogue of just Mrs. Wilson, young Johnny's mother

"Johnny, you're late. Come in and get your lunch."

"Boyd? I don't believe I've met Boyd. Bring him in, dear, since you've invited him for lunch."

"Johnny, that's not very polite to either your friend or your mother. Come sit down, Boyd." (As she turns to show Boyd where to sit, she sees that he is a Negro boy, about Johnny's age but smaller.)

"Johnny, what did you make Boyd do?"

"You shouldn't let Johnny make you carry all that wood. Sit down now and eat lunch, both of you."

"Johnny, go on and eat your lunch."

"Are you hungry, Boyd?"

"Well, don't you let Johnny stop you. He always fusses about eating, so you just see that you get a good lunch. There's plenty of food here for you to have all you want."

"**Doesn't** eat tomatoes, Johnny. And just because you don't like them, don't say that about Boyd. Boyd will eat **anything**."

"Boyd wants to grow up and be a big strong man so he can work hard. I'll bet Boyd's father eats stewed tomatoes."

"I'll bet he's strong, though. (Hesitating) Does he . . . work?"

"There, you see? And he certainly has to be strong to do that—all that lifting and carrying at a factory."

(Feeling defeated) "What does your mother do, Boyd?"

"Oh. She doesn't work, then?"

"You really don't want any stewed tomatoes, Boyd?"

"That's a very fine attitude for her to have, Boyd. I imagine you're all very proud of her." (She then restrains an impulse to pat Boyd on the head.)

"What about all your other brothers and sisters? I guess all of you want to make just as much of yourselves as you can."

"Now eat as much as you want to, Boyd. I want to see you get filled up."

(Taking a deep breath) "Boyd, Johnny has some suits that are a little too small for him, and a winter coat. It's not new, of course, but there's lots of wear in it still. And I have a few dresses that your mother and sister could probably use. Your mother can make them over into lots of things for all of you, and I'd be very happy to give them to you. Suppose before you leave I make up a big bundle and then you and Johnny can take it over to your mother right away . . . ." (Her voice trails off as she sees the puzzled expression on Boyd's face.)

(Lifting a plate of gingerbread off the table as Boyd is about to take another piece) "There are many little boys like you, Boyd, who would be very grateful for the clothes someone was kind enough to give them."

"Don't think I'm angry, Boyd. I'm just disappointed in you, that's all. Now let's not say anything more about it."

(And coming up, the dialogue of Mrs. Wilson's son, Johnny)

Sequenced dialogue of just Mrs. Wilson's son, Johnny

"Just a minute, Mother. After you, my dear Alphonse."

"Mother, I brought Boyd home for lunch with me."

"Boyd! Hey, Boyd, come on in!"

"Well, hurry, or my mother'll be sore."

"Why shouldn't he carry the wood, Mother? It's his wood. We got it at his place."

"Sure (holding out the dish of scrambled eggs Mrs. Wilson has made to Boyd), after you, my dear Alphonse."

"After **you**, my dear Alphonse."

"Boyd don't eat tomatoes, do you, Boyd?" (as Mrs. Wilson puts a dish of stewed tomatoes beside Boyd's plate)

"Bet he won't."

"So does mine. Sometimes he doesn't eat hardly anything. He's a little guy, though. Wouldn't hurt a flea."

"Sure, Boyd's father works in a factory."

"I guess so."

"Boyd's father doesn't have to. He's a foreman."

"No, thank you, Mrs. Wilson, no thank you, Mrs. Wilson, no thank you, Mrs. Wilson."

"Boyd's sister's going to work, though. She's going to be a teacher."

"We're going to be tank drivers, Boyd and me. Zoom."

"Boyd eats a lot, but not as much as I do. I'm bigger than he is."

"We don't have time to carry that old stuff around, Mother. We got to play tanks with the kids today."

"Boyd will take them if you want him to, Mother."

"'Bye, Mother."

"After you, my dear Alphonse."

"I don't know. She's screwy sometimes."

(And coming up, the dialogue of Johnny Wilson's friend Boyd)

Sequenced dialogue of just Johnny Wilson's friend Boyd

*"No, after **you**, my dear Alphonse."*

"I'm coming. Just got to unload this stuff. Where'll I put this stuff, Johnny?" (The "stuff" is split kindling wood that both his arms are filled with.)

"How do you do, Mrs. Wilson?"

*"After **you**, my dear Alphonse."*

"Thank you, Mrs. Wilson."

"Mine's a little guy, too."

"My father eats anything he wants to."

(Surprised) "My mother? She takes care of us kids."

"Why should she? You don't work?"

"No, thank you, Mrs. Wilson."

"There's only Jean and me. I don't know yet what I want to be when I grow up."

"You're not much bigger. I can beat you running."

"But I have plenty of clothes, thank you. And I don't think my mother knows how to sew very well, and anyway I guess we buy about everything we need. Thank you very much, though."

"I didn't mean to make you mad, Mrs. Wilson."

(Standing up to leave but staring for a minute at Mrs. Wilson's back before going through the door that Johnny has opened; in a low voice asking) "Is your mother still mad?"

"So's mine." (Hesitating) "After **you**, my dear Alphonse."

What Do You Think?

After *You*, My Dear Reader:
Here's a Lot of Thinking About Thinking—to Think About—
(So Take as Much Time—Over Time—as You Want)

- what instances of stereotyping and prejudice do you find in the dialogue of the three characters in Shirley Jackson's short story "After You, My Dear Alphonse"? What is the nature of the stereotyping and prejudice?
- an early assumption that Mrs. Wilson makes is that Johnny made Boyd carry the wood. Why do you think she makes this particular assumption?
- find other examples of assumptive thinking on the part of Mrs. Wilson, and explain their nature. Who is the character in the story that corrects these assumptions and what specific evidence or proof does that character provide?
- what is the basic overall assumption that Mrs. Wilson makes throughout the story—the assumption that takes in all of her other assumptions? Try stating Mrs. Wilson's overall assumption in the form of a generalization,

- why does Mrs. Wilson hesitate before asking Boyd whether his father works?

- why does Mrs. Wilson feel "defeated" after Johnny explains that the work Boyd's father does in the factory does not include lifting and carrying because Boyd's father is a factory foreman?

- how would you explain the "oh" in Mrs. Wilson's comment about Boyd's mother, "Oh. She doesn't work, then?"

- analyze and comment on the phrasing Mrs. Wilson makes use of when she says, "What about all your other brothers and sisters? I guess all of you want to make just as much of yourselves as you can,"

- after Boyd states that his sister is "going to be a teacher," Mrs. Wilson responds, "That's a very fine attitude for her to have, Boyd." Comment on Mrs. Wilson's choice of the word "attitude,"

- after her comment about Boyd's sister, why, in your opinion, does Mrs. Wilson have an impulse to pat Boyd on the head, and why does she restrain herself by pulling back?

- comment on both the deep breath Mrs. Wilson takes before she begins to talk about the hand-me-down clothing and on Boyd's puzzled expression as she speaks,

- what does Mrs. Wilson mean by the phrase "boys like you" when she says, "There are many little boys like you, Boyd, who would be very grateful for the clothes someone was kind enough to give them"?

- what was it, do you think, that caused Boyd to realize that Mrs. Wilson was "mad" at him? What was it that got Mrs. Wilson "mad"?

- why do you think the story's author, Shirley Jackson, makes a point of writing that before he left the Wilson house, Boyd "stood for a minute, staring at Mrs. Wilson's back"?

- the following exchange of dialogue between Johnny and Boyd occupies what is an important position in any story—near the end: Johnny says of his mother, "She's screwy, sometimes" and Boyd responds, "So's mine." Explain how this brief exchange between the two boys captures a major point that the entire story is making about stereotyping. Compare this exchange with an earlier one in which Boyd says, "My father eats anything he wants to" and Johnny responds, "So does mine,"
- comment on why you think the author, at the very end of the story, has Boyd hesitate before he says the exact same words that he and Johnny have said so many times before: "After *you*, my dear Alphonse,"
- as a reader of short stories, comment on whether you find this particular short story to be up-to-date or dated or a mixture of the two,
- comment on whether you find this particular story to be realistic, unrealistic, exaggerated but believable, exaggerated and unbelievable,
- as a reader, good thinker, and human being, how can you personally guard against being prejudiced? How can you keep yourself from slipping into negative or hurtful stereotypes?

Mind Set

Qualities of Good Thinkers—
and Selected Dialogue, For the Last Time,
from the Play "Twelve Angry Men"

So far in this chapter we have seen that good thinkers are alert to bias or prejudice, try to avoid thinking in stereotypes, and are careful to examine assumptions they might be making.

In earlier chapters, we came to realize that good thinkers work to consciously think about the thinking they do and try to be open-minded and broad-minded.

In order to come up with an even more complete picture of the kind of thinking good thinkers do, let's take one last look at the thoughts of fully seven of the twelve jurors from the play "Twelve Angry Men." As you re-read their dialogue quoted below (which has been grouped by the juror who is speaking), focus on what it is specifically that each juror is mentally doing that makes him either a good thinker or not a good thinker.

What Do You Think?

Based on what you have just been asked to focus on in the Mind Set above, compile in your personal journal as complete a list as you can of the "desirable do's" and the "definite don'ts" for all good thinkers.

> **Juror 1:** Maybe if the gentleman who's disagreeing (that's Juror 8, who was the first to vote "not guilty") . . . could tell us why. You know, tell us what he thinks, we could show him where he's probably mixed up.

> **Juror 8 (responding):** I sat there in court for six days listening while the evidence built up. You know everybody sounded so positive that I started to get a peculiar feeling about this trial. I mean, nothing is *that* positive. I had questions I would have liked to ask. Maybe they wouldn't have meant anything. I don't know.

> **Juror 8 (later in the play):** I don't know whether I believe it (the defendant's story) or not. Maybe I don't.

Juror 8 (speaking to Juror 9 about Juror 7's walking away from him): He can't hear you. He never will.

Juror 2: Well, it's hard to put into words. I just . . . think he's guilty. I thought it was obvious from the word go.

Juror 3 (speaking to Juror 8): Well, look, do you really think he's innocent?

Juror 4: I don't see any need for arguing like this. I think we ought to be able to behave like gentlemen.

Juror 4: If we're going to discuss the case, let's discuss the facts.

Juror 9 (speaking directly to Juror 10): Do you think you were born with a monopoly on the truth?

Juror 9 (changing his vote from "guilty" to "not guilty"): The boy on trial is probably guilty. But I want to hear more. Right now the vote is ten to two.

Juror 11: I don't believe I must be loyal to one side or the other. I'm simply asking questions.

Assessing Your Thinking

Some Do's and Don'ts of Good Thinking

- make a list of what you have discovered that good thinkers try to do,
- make a second list of what it is that good thinkers try to avoid doing,

- compare your lists of "desirable do's" and "definite don'ts" for good thinkers with the lists that appear on the following pages.

Reflections

The Kinds of Things Good Thinkers Make a Point of Doing

Here are some examples of the kinds of things that good thinkers learn to do and work to implement with any content:

- recognize that there are things that they don't know;
- hesitate stating definitively (often referred to as "pointing out") that "It's a fact that . . . ," when they have not given any thought as to whether it might not be;
- admit it when they don't know something;
- admit it when they are not sure of something;
- ask questions;
- try to find out as much information as possible before forming an opinion;
- keep an open mind to new ideas and other people's points of view;
- have a genuine interest in other people's opinions;
- try to be as broad-minded as possible;
- realize that what they think is obvious is not always obvious to others, or to any single individual all the time;
- base their ideas and opinions on up-to-date knowledge of scientifically or experentially established facts;
- distinguish between beliefs or intuitions and facts and fact-based opinions;
- think about why they think what they think (have reasons for their ideas and viewpoints);

- think about how they came to think what they think (think about the act and process of thinking);
- tend to be skeptical in a way that is not off-putting or confrontational;
- try not to come across in their overall attitude or in their specific opinions as cynical;
- understand the difference between things that are possible, things that are probable or likely, and things that are certain or definite (for the time being);
- try to be aware of their assumptions (first realizing that they are bound to have some);
- make a periodic point of re-examining their assumptions.

Reflections

The Kinds of Things Good Thinkers Work to Avoid Doing

Here are some examples of the kinds of things that good thinkers try to avoid doing whatever the content and that you can begin to unlearn if you need to:

- open their mouths before they open their minds (the "knee-jerk" equivalent for the mouth—a "jaw jerk");
- take a side in a disagreement and stay loyal to it no matter what (as is expected in a formal debate, where winning the debate, not necessarily finding out the truth, is the goal);
- think they know it all (and come across to others as a "know-it-all");
- think that others don't know anything;
- narrow or close their minds to new ideas and different points of view;
- take things for granted;

- never question their beliefs;
- never examine their "gut feelings";
- fail to distinguish between belief and knowledge;
- take on faith matters that need to be factually examined;
- allow their emotions to rule—or over-rule—their thinking;
- get frustrated or angry when others disagree with what they are saying;
- view other people and situations through bias or prejudice;
- let others do their thinking for them.

Mind Set

In Conclusion

Our individual assumptions often arise from our belief that "the majority rules" and that if there is "general agreement" on something, then that something has, of course, to be correct. Good thinkers know that it is extremely rare that any group of people regularly and repeatedly assesses its assumptions; the truth is that what keeps these group or societal assumptions alive and active is little more than historical continuity coupled with inertia.

Good thinkers also know that they are not "know-it-alls." If it is true, as American President Abraham Lincoln said (in part) that "you can fool some of the people some of the time," it stands to reason that some of these people who occasionally get fooled are good thinkers. The real fool, as part of a famous saying puts it (you could look it up in almost any book of quotations), is the person who "knows not—and knows not that he knows not."

Assessing Your Thinking

Get Out Your Journal and Think Through Your Writing

Think a bit about all three choices below and, then, in your personal journal, try writing—at length—on at least one of them:

- reflect on your own experiences with "us" and "them" thinking, negative prejudice, or stereotyping. Were you on the giving end or the receiving end?
- reflect on your own experiences with mistaken assumptions (assumptive thinking). Were you on the giving end or the receiving end?
- react to the following comments about jurors who are or are not good thinkers made by a university professor of psychology: "Better reasoners weigh all of a conflicting body of evidence against multiple theories (of what happened)—a process that leads away from the extreme theories represented by opposing lawyers' closing arguments; less capable jurors more readily settle on one theory, ignore evidence that doesn't fit, and never consider alternatives."

4

Thinking in Generalizations

Think About It

In this chapter you will discover:

- how generalizations work,
- why, generally speaking, it is essential to be able to think, speak, and write in generalizations,
- why it is important to examine the truth or falsity of our generalizations.

Mind Set

Generally Speaking

The fictional mother, Mrs. Wilson, that you met in Chapter 3 in Shirley Jackson's short story "After You, My Dear Alphonse," is blind to Boyd, her son Johnny's friend, because she "sees" him completely in terms of her many stereotypes about black people. As she "sees" it, Boyd must be poor, and needy, and always hungry. Boyd's father, if in the unlikely possibility that Boyd has a father at home who can keep a job, must be a physical laborer whose low wages can barely support what must be a large family. And that family would, of course, have few possessions of value, and would, most certainly, be grateful for any of Mrs. Wilson's (or anyone else's) hand-me-down clothing.

Why must all the "musts" and certainties of the above paragraph be true? The answer, of course, is that they don't have to be—and in the particular instance of Boyd and his family, they're not. Mrs. Wilson is, in actual fact, a storehouse of stereotypes when it comes to black people; she has so conditioned her mind to see black people in a certain way that she is only momentarily puzzled when Boyd corrects her with the facts *particular* to him and his family; then Mrs. Wilson pushes on, quick to grab from the stocked shelves of her mind the next stereotype she can put her fingers on.

Mrs. Wilson's way of thinking through stereotypes certainly sounds like the kind of thinking you would not want to model your own thinking on, and that, of course, is one of the main points of Shirley Jackson's short story. Yet, thinking in stereotypes is an example of a kind of thinking that we human beings would be less human for if we had to do without it.

This kind of thinking is known as thinking in generalizations. To understand the nature of this essential human ability and the problems that arise when our unexamined generalizations are stereotypes is the purpose and focus of this chapter.

We often hear people use the phrases "in general" or "generally speaking" or just "generally"—and not give them that much thought because they are so common to our language. But what does it actually mean to think in generalizations—and why is generalizing so important an element in good thinking?

Generalizations—or general statements—are statements that say something about *all things of a certain kind—without exception.* Thinking and then speaking in a general way is tremendously empowering because it enables you to make statements that are all-encompassing, or defining, or characteristic about an entire group of people or things.

When we generalize, we group people or things together in order to express the same thing about all of them in one single statement; this is quite economical. Generalizations are born when we notice something about a particular person or object and then notice the very same thing about another person or object.

What Do You Think?

- generally speaking, how do you feel about what you have just read?
- do *any specific exceptions* to your general feeling about what you read in this chapter's opening Mind Set occur to you at the moment?
- try making a general statement about how a generalization might be considered to be "like a large umbrella" used to keep your body from getting wet in a rain storm.

Reflections

Generalizations as "Umbrella" Thinking

Our thinking in generalizations—and, therefore, our speaking and writing—is sort of like using an umbrella that is large enough to protect us from a heavy rain. We take the umbrella for granted; its size and shape make sense to us for the purpose we plan to put it to. In fact, we would laugh out loud if someone suggested we carry, instead, separate small umbrellas to cover our face, and our left shoulder, and our right shoulder, and the better part of our back. Because generalizations are "large" and cover quite a bit of informational territory, they make it easier, and simpler, and more economical to think about our world, speak about our world, write about our word—in short, to make sense of our world.

Mind Set

Generalizations About Large and Small Groups of Things

Let's say, for example, that we want to make a generalization about "buildings." Our statement, then, would not only be saying something about office buildings and factories (two kinds of buildings) but also about houses (a third kind of building). In fact, our generalization about buildings would be saying something about any and all of those structures (like office buildings, factories, houses, hospitals, and schools) that we commonly name with the label "a building."

Here's an example of a possible generalization: "Buildings are structures with walls, floors, and ceilings."

This generalization about buildings, however, says nothing about bridges, for example. Although bridges are a kind of structure, bridges are not among those structures we commonly think of, or refer to, as buildings.

Let's suppose, now, that we want to make a generalization about the particular kinds of buildings known as office buildings. Here's an example of a possible generalization: "Office buildings are made for people to work in."

This generalization about office buildings, however, says nothing, for example, about prisons. Although people do engage in work in prisons, we don't commonly think of prisons as places of work; in other words, their *defining characteristic* is not "a place *for* people to work in." Instead, we think of prisons as either places of punishment or places of rehabilitation (and we haven't, in this country, thought about them as places of rehabilitation for quite a long time).

But let's release ourselves from prison and return to our examination of "buildings" and "office buildings"; while both of these "place names" encompass generalizations, the first one essentially deals with (and therefore names) a larger group of items than the second—there are more buildings, in general, than there are office buildings, and so whenever we talk about "buildings" we are also, automatically, talking about "office buildings (since office buildings are included in the group or category known as "buildings"). Any generalization about "buildings" will always be more inclusive than any generalization about "office buildings."

In the field of mathematics (and I can almost feel your anxiety level rising at the mention of *that* field, as though the study of language and thinking were not difficult enough!), we would say that "office buildings" is a *subset* of the *set* "buildings." This "something-within-something-else" idea is often expressed pictorially (in a sketch or drawing like the one below).

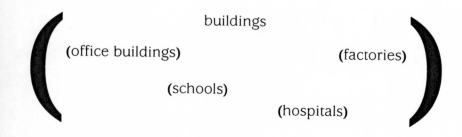

The larger circle, labeled "buildings," contains the smaller circle labeled "office buildings," as well as other small circles that name other kinds of buildings. See, no reason to be all that anxious about the language of mathematics.

What Do You Think?

- can the title of the play "Twelve Angry Men" be considered a generalization?
- explain why you do or do not think so.

Reflections

They're *All* Angry

If we were to take the title "Twelve Angry Men" and re-write it as a general statement, we might produce a generalization like this one: "The twelve men on the jury of this trial are angry." This particular statement about the twelve jurors qualifies as a generalization because it states something about "all things of a certain kind—without exception." It says that the twelve men who make up this particular jury are angry—all of them. Because this generalization speaks about a very small number of people—only twelve—out of the world's total population, this generalization is not overwhelmingly inclusive; however, it is still a legitimate generalization.

What Do You Think?

- were you anxious about using a kind of mathematics to answer the preceding question? Why is that? How "mathematical" did the thinking that you did feel?

- which "thing of a certain kind" is more inclusive—"human beings" or "people in this room"?
- why do you feel you're "right" about your answer?

Reflections

More or Less Inclusive Groups

We can make generalizations about "human beings" and we can make generalizations about "the people in this room." There's pretty much nothing to stop us.

Both "human beings" and "the people in this room" are "things of a certain kind." However, our first generalization would always be much more inclusive than our second even if this room were to be filled to capacity with people (wall-to-wall people, floor-to-ceiling people). In fact, in order for the number of people in this room to be simply equal to the number of human beings existing, we would have to declare that by "this room" we were, in both a prosaically (prose-like) definitional way as well as a fairly poetic way, referring to the planet Earth.

Mind Set

True and False Generalizations

It is possible that some of you (definitely not all of you!) in your reading about generalizations so far in this chapter may have slipped into some assumptive thinking: you may have assumed that all generalizations are true. We will not, however, send you directly back to Chapter 3 (do *not* pass Go; do *not* collect $200!); instead, let's examine right here and now the assumption that "all generalizations are true."

No doubt as soon as you heard that statement in your mind, you realized that "all generalizations are true" is, itself, a nice example of a generalization; it says something ("they are true") about all things of a certain kind (generalizations). Interestingly, this particular generalization about generalizations is *not* true, but false.

Mind Set

A True Generalization About Inclusive Groups

To begin to understand why the generalization "all generalizations are true" is a false generalization, you will not need any math. (Sighs of relief to be heard in the background?) Instead, let's go back to that fairly inclusive group known as "human beings" and make a new—and true—generalization about that group: "human beings are mortal."

Reflections

Good Thinking and True Generalizations

To be "mortal" means to die—eventually, while to be "immortal" (its antonym or opposite) means to be "not mortal," which would mean that you live forever. Thus, the meaning of the generalization "human beings are mortal" is that all those "things" known as "human beings" eventually die. This particular generalization turns out to be true. Based on all known available evidence, it is true that, so far, all people do die no matter how long they have lived.

A generalization, we have already discovered (perhaps to our surprise), can be false. Nevertheless, it is still a generalization in its essence, structure, and nature. It's just a generalization that turns out not to be true.

What Do You Think?

Let's examine this generalization: "American automobile drivers observe posted speed limits." Is this a true or false generalization?

Reflections

It's Either One or the Other

It's a false generalization. For proof, we can point to arrest and conviction records across the country that show that there are, actually, a number of automobile drivers in the United States who have exceeded a posted speed limit.

If this one generalization about American automobile drivers is demonstrably false, then it follows logically that the generalization "all generalizations are true" cannot be true and, therefore, must be false. Why? Because—and, sorry, but get ready for the math—it takes only "one exception" to a generalization for that generalization to fail the "lie-detector test." We call this one exception a "counter-example" ("counter," like its related form "contra," means "against")—and all it takes is a single exception to a generalization to establish the falsity of that generalization. For any generalization to be true, it must be completely and totally and all-the-time true. Zero counter-examples.

Since generalizations are *either* true *or* false (but not both or neither), good thinkers realize the importance of knowing which ones are which. Good thinkers not only watch what they say when they speak in generalizations, but they watch what others say, in general, to check out the truth or falsity of their thinking.

Mind Set

A False Generalization About Inclusive Groups

Let's go back, again, to that group known as "human beings" (a helpful group to have on hand) and make, this time, a false generalization about "human beings": "Human beings have brown eyes."

Reflections

Good Thinking and False Generalizations

Although we are still generalizing about that fairly inclusive group known as "human beings," this particular generalization does not bear up under scrutiny. Clearly, all we need to do is to point out human beings whose eyes are blue, or green, or some color other than brown. These exceptions to the generalization make the generalization false. It is still a generalization, but it is a false one. (And, remembering the power of the counter-example, it only takes the existence of one blue-eyed person, for example, to prove it.)

Mind Set

True and False Generalizations About Less Inclusive Groups

Here's an example of a generalization about that less inclusive group known as "the people in this room": "The people in this room are wearing eyeglasses."

Reflections

Eyeing "The People in This Room"

This generalization about "the people in this room" takes in and says something about fewer individuals than our earlier generalization about "human beings." Despite the fact that this generalization is about a much, much smaller group, it still says something about every single member of the group it refers to. And if you want to see who the members of this group are, just take a look around *the room you are in right now*, and remember that the generalization is saying the following about all the members of this group: they have eyeglasses on at this very moment.

What Do You Think?

Is the generalization true or false? How do you know for a fact?

Reflections

A Consensus Opinion?

Only *you* can answer definitively. To find out the truth or falsity of this particular generalization, you need to take a good look *right away* (for evidence!) at the faces of everyone in the room that you're in right now. As for you yourself, either reach up and touch your eyes or look in the nearest mirror because, in case you didn't notice, you are one of "the people in this room."

What Do You Think?

Will all of the "yous" that are reading this book and conducting this experiment come to the same conclusion—be in agreement, arrive at a consensus of opinion? Give as many reasons as you can for your answer.

Reflections

Changing Realties Can Produce Changed Generalizations

But why must you do all this *right away*? Here's why: in a matter of moments, the truth or falsity of this generalization about the people in this room could change. "How could that be?" you might be asking (it's a good question for good thinkers to be asking). And why don't you venture several guesses before you read on. (Guesses are good, as in "good thinking.")

Assessing Your Thinking

Among the "hows" that you came up with, did you think of some of the following? Someone with or without glasses on could enter the room. Someone with glasses on could take their glasses off (for any reason whatsoever): to rub their eyes, to look at their glasses to see whether there's something wrong with them because they caught you staring at them, you name it. Someone not wearing glasses could reach for the dirty pair in their pocket and put them on to see just how dirty they are. (Because contact lenses are not generally included in the category named and defined as "eyeglasses," they do not figure in this generalization and, thus, do not count.)

What Do You Think?

- make a true generalization about buildings,
- make a true generalization about a particular type of building,

- make a false generalization about a particular type of building and explain how and why it is false,
- make a true generalization about the people in the room you are in right now (regardless of how many of them there are),
- make a false generalization about the people in the room you are in right now (regardless of how many of them there are), and explain how and why it is false,
- make a true generalization about human beings,
- make a false generalization about human beings, and explain how and why it is false,
- name a very inclusive group or category; then make a true generalization about it,
- make a false generalization about that same very inclusive group or category, and explain how and why it is false,
- make a true generalization about a different, less inclusive group or category (for ideas, look around you at home, at work, at play, outdoors),
- make a false generalization about that same less inclusive group or category, and explain how and why it is false,
- explain in your journal how the definition of "a generalization" is itself a generalization (the definition of a generalization, you will remember, states that "a generalization is a statement that says something about all the things of a certain kind, without exception").

Mind Set

From Generalization to Paradox

Hold on, what's a "paradox"? According to a very old and very bad joke, a paradox is "two ducks" (a "pair of ducks"). How's that for a good example of the category "very bad jokes"? A dictionary that makes no use of humorous punchlines might define a "paradox" as . . . . But wait; let's hold off with a formal dictionary definition for now. Instead, here's an anecdote to ponder:

Back in the fourth century B.C. (*before* the *common* era), the Greek philosopher Euboulides found himself thinking about a generalization that had been made by Epimenides the Cretan (a Cretan was a citizen of the Greek island of Crete). Epimenides had said: "All Cretans are liars." Euboulides found himself wondering whether Epimenides was telling the truth." Can you see why?

What Do You Think?

- was Epimenides telling the truth—or was he lying when he said that "all Cretans are liars"? Explain your reasoning out loud or in your personal journal,
- either out loud or in your journal, talk about any difficulty you had in deciding whether you thought Epimenides was being truthful or not,
- in the anecdote about Epimenides's statement, the wording of the statement produces an excellent example of "a paradox"; write down in your journal how you would define "paradox" based on your experience with just this particular example of one,
- how close is your definition to the following dictionary definition: "a paradox is a statement that seems to contradict itself"?
- if you are mathematically inclined, explain how "sets" and "subsets" could be used to help someone understand the nature of a paradox,
- whether you are mathematically inclined or not (but seem to have grasped the essential nature of a paradox), prove that to the rest of us by trying your hand at creating at least

two paradoxes (two separate and unrelated paradoxical statements),

- in your journal, write about what is going on in a generalization that is also a paradox between the maker of the generalization and the things that are being generalized about.

Mind Set

From Generalization to Stereotype

Although the particular false generalization considered earlier in this chapter—"human beings have brown eyes"—appears to be a fairly harmless general statement, it is possible that someone could use it in a dangerous and hurtful way to create significant personal or societal damage.

Reflections

How Stereotypes Are Born

Let's suppose that someone—Person A—has had a really bad experience with, you guessed it, Person B, an individual who, quite incidentally, happens to have blue eyes. "A," for spite, wants to get back at "B," so "A" decides to "spread the word" that "human beings have brown eyes."

If "A" repeats this false generalization long enough and frequently enough, and gets other people to "buy into it" and take up the cause, some individuals in society may begin to think that having brown eyes is essential to what it means to be a human being. (That's because, as you probably remember, generalizations are considered to be all-encompassing, defining, and characteristic.)

Therefore, it could logically be concluded from this generalization that any person with non-brown eyes (anyone *different in that respect*) is not human—or at least not completely or truly human.

As you can see, what has happened here is that "A" has gotten back at "B" by creating a negative prejudice and stereotype about an entire group of individuals (all non-brown-eyed people) by promulgating and popularizing the generalization that "true" human beings all have brown eyes. This negative prejudice and stereotype against blue-eyed people, green-eyed people, and others of "them" could easily get transformed into active discrimination against "them" and in favor of "us of the brown eyes."

This "transformation" could, and would, occur in many areas of social life, for example, in civil rights, marriage rights, housing, education, and most other personal and social relationships. At best, some of "them" (they would be referred to as "the few good ones among 'em") would be "tolerated" (in the sense of "put up with"); at worst, all of "them" would be persecuted.

What Do You Think?

- in your journal, reflect on how a false generalization or stereotype about a particular group can pose a danger to members of that group,
- in your journal, discuss as many examples as you can from world history, from American history, from your neighborhood's history, from your family's history, and from your own personal history of how a false generalization or stereotype was hurtful or harmful to a particular group of people,
- the following statement has popularly come to be called "the Mozart Effect" (named after the classical music composer

Wolfgang Amadeus Mozart): "When classical music is played to young school children it makes their brains work better"; what makes this statement a generalization, how inclusive is the generalization, and how would you go about determining the truth or falsity of this generalization?

Mind Set

In Conclusion

Good thinkers understand that thinking in generalizations is a powerful way to make sense of a world of information (often "too much information!") and a powerful way to make sense of life; at the same time, good thinkers recognize the dangers lurking in unexamined generalizations and their potential for hurtful and harmful stereotyping. Such "sweeping generalizations" are more like a vacuum cleaner that sucks much too much in to be effective than a broom that sweeps some connected things into a neat and manageable pile.

Assessing Your Thinking

A Journal Entry

Write a journal entry in which you reflect on the material and activities about "generalizations" presented in this chapter.

Assessing Your Thinking

A Journal Entry Inspires A Short Story

Write a different journal entry, this time about a true experience you have had in which a person behaved in a way that showed both a belief in a false generalization and a narrow or relatively closed mind. The person can be anyone from your personal history—a friend, a family member or relative, an acquaintance, a classmate or teacher from your school days, a neighbor, anyone—even yourself. Be as specific as you can about all the individuals involved in the incident, about what happened, and about how the person's belief in a false generalization and the person's narrow-mindedness was revealed.

After you have completed your journal entry, read it over to yourself out loud and think about how you could take some of what you wrote and make use of it in an original short story. The purpose of the story would be to tell—in narrative (tale-telling) form—about a time when your main character acted in such a way in a particular situation to reveal both a belief in a false generalization and the trait of narrow-mindedness or close-mindedness.

To help you get started writing the structure of your narrative, do not be embarrassed to begin your rough draft of a short story with a formula opening such as "once there was a . . . ," or "I remember the time that . . . ," or "the story is told of . . ." (sound familiar?), or even (yes!) "once upon a time . . . ." (You can change your formula opening to a more original one when you are ready to revise your rough draft.)

Although this activity may sound daunting to you right now, once you get going, you'll see that it's not. In fact, generally speaking, it's a lot of fun.

5

Thinking Through Categories

Think About It

In this chapter you will discover:

- why it is that you know more than you think you do,
- what categories are—and how you can use them to help you recall factual information and memorize (by rote!) new sets of facts,
- how thinking through categories enables you to order, organize, and process your thinking, your speaking, and your writing.

Mind Set

Being Mindful

The story is told of the man (but it also could be a woman) who insisted that he never forgot anything he had learned or experienced.

Perfect memory. Total recall.

"It's true," the man (or woman) would proclaim to anyone who would listen: "I have an incredible memory; I can't think of anything I have ever forgotten."

A good friend asked (gently): "But what about all the things you have forgotten that you don't remember forgetting?"

What Do You Think?

- does the man (or woman) have a "perfect memory" or "total recall"? Tell why you do or do not think so,
- paraphrase, which is to say, put the sense of what you've learned into *your own words*, what the point is that the friend is making,
- think about the different meanings of the word "incredible"; take the time to consult a dictionary if you can't, on your own, come up with two *rather different* meanings (hint: the root or stem "cred" means "believe"),
- how is it a false statement that the man (or woman) has a memory that is "incredible"?
- how is it a true statement that the man (or woman) has a memory that is "incredible"?
- what do you find interesting about the phrasing of the statement "I can't think of anything I have ever forgotten"?

Reflections

Try to Remember

In one of the most remembered and memorable of American off-Broadway musicals, "The Fantastics," a wise character sings:

"Try to remember the kind of September when . . . (insert special remembrance here)—and if you remember, then follow, follow, follow, follow, follow, follow, follow, follow, follow, follow."

The ten (maybe it was only nine, who remembers for sure?) "follows" do a good, though noticeably repetitive, job of getting across the idea that someone will be in the perfect position to follow the thinking of someone else if first, before any following can commence, the two agree on the details of a particular, perhaps shared, memory.

Not only do no two people remember the "same" thing in exactly the same way (or even-all-that-close-to way), but when one of them forgets having experienced or learned something, he or she may also forget the forgetting. (Interestingly, when some people say "I don't remember *that* at all" about something someone else has remembered concerning the two of them, the second person is often implying either that the first person's memory is somewhat faulty or that the thing "remembered" never actually even happened.)

Here's a true generalization we'd like to make right about now: "People forget—and they sometimes forget that they forgot."

This does not mean that we no longer know these forgotten things; it's more like, for the time being, we don't know that we know them.

For example: did you ever have something—let's say a toy when you were a child—then lose it and, later on, forget you ever had it as one of your toys? Then, one day, that particular toy turns up, and perhaps you say, "Oh, look, here's that toy I lost; good grief, it was so long ago, I forgot all about it!"

Or, that toy may actually wind up being lost for good—both as a possession of yours and as a memory; in that case, you will literally have nothing to say about it because as far as you know (which is only as far as you can remember), that toy—of yours—never existed.

Or, lastly, simply the memory of that particular toy may surface at some future point in time—but not the toy itself. Perhaps you'll say, "Remember that great wind-up toy dog Dad gave me on my fourth birthday? I wonder whatever happened to it."

In the 2013 novel LIFE AFTER LIFE, by Kate Atkinson, the mother in the story is planning a surprise birthday party for her youngest child and only son, Teddy. One of the woman's daughters, Pamela, complains about never having had a surprise birthday party herself—but the mother quickly corrects her: "Of course you have, you just don't remember." The narrative continues: "Was this true? Pamela frowned at the impossibility of knowing."

What Do You Think?

- explain "the impossibility of knowing" in the Mind Set above,
- can you come up with similar instances of remembrance or non-remembrance that you have had in you life or know about from others? Try to remember! Try really hard. It may help you to invoke the Greek goddess of memory, whose name, if memory serves, was Mnemosyne; if you look at Mnemosyne's name—the opening "M" is silent—you can probably see why out loud "sound" techniques for remembering things are called "mnemonic" devices.

(Alliteration, the repetition of the opening consonant *sound*—not the *letter* of the alphabet, necessarily, because, for example, both the letter "f" and the letters "ph" can make the same sound, but the *actual sound heard* when the opening letter or letters are pronounced—of two or more words is a well-known mnemonic device used by good thinkers. The repetition of the "puh" sound in the following helps your memory recall both this opening line and the other alliterative lines that follow it: "Peter Piper picked a peck of pickled peppers . . . .")

- once you remember, then "follow, follow, follow, follow, follow, follow, follow, follow, follow, follow" up with an entry in your personal journal on wherever your memory takes you in your thinking.

Mind Set

You Know More Than You Think You Remember

One result of the complex relationship between what we have learned and experienced and what we remember is that some of us think we know very little about some subject or other when, actually, we know more than we think we do. The "more" is what we have forgotten that we know, what we have "lost" for the moment (or longer) from our memory. However, what's lost may be—and often is—found. Sometimes we accidentally come upon some of these forgotten things in our mind when we are thinking of something else (they come to mind!); other times, a memory is "on the tip of our tongue" but, unfortunately, try as hard as we do, we can't get it out of our mouth (because it is really still stuck in our mind).

Similarly, some people who are searching for an actual object or item they have misplaced will, later on, while they are looking for "another something" whose location they have temporarily forgotten—well, guess what they (accidentally or not) stumble upon. Would you believe, the first thing they misplaced? You would believe it, because it probably has happened to you!

You would probably also agree that mentally (neurologically, psychologically) "stumbling upon" what we used to know but later forgot is a pretty "hit-or-miss" approach to "knowing once again," which is literally what the word "recognize" means. (Still have that dictionary nearby? The prefix "re" means "before" and the stem or root "cog" means knowledge from thinking, as in words like recognize, cogitate, and cognitive.) No wonder we experience the shock of recognition when we come upon something from our past and can say, "I know that!"

Clearly, good thinkers need—and, of course, have—a more systematic approach to "total recall." That system involves "thinking through categories."

What Do You Think?

Try the following experiment:

- how many birds do you think you can name off the top of your head? Write that number down,
- begin listing birds by name. Stop only when you think that you simply cannot think of another single one; then, count the number of names and compare the total with the number you originally thought you could name. Did you name more than you thought you could?

- if you didn't name more than you thought you could, tell why you think you didn't,
- if you did name more than you originally thought you would be able to, tell why you think you succeeded beyond your expectations; are you aware of having used, while you were naming the birds, any system, method, strategy, technique, or trick? If so, tell about your awareness,
- regardless of whether you exceeded your expectations or not, try to think of a way you could add to the number you reached; for help in coming up with a way, look over your list of names for any connections, or patterns, or relationships and see whether you can discover a way that naming one bird might lead you into naming another and then another and then another.

Mind Set

"Justlikethat"

No matter how many birds you succeeded in naming, try this: look at your list of names to see whether there are any places where three or four bird names came to mind for you "justlikethat" (with thanks to the American poet E. E. Cummings, or e. e. cummings, as he preferred, who created "justlikethat" in a poem of his about Buffalo Bill to both verbally and visually convey the incredible speed of that marksman's shooting of pigeons).

What Do You Think?

Can you figure out why this "justlikethat" sequence happened, why your mind thought so quickly at that particular point?

Reflections

Thinking Through Categories

Your "justlikethat" experiences were not at all like "stumbling around" in your mind until you tripped over something you'd forgotten. Nor were they about waiting until whatever memory was on the tip of your tongue fell off it and into the audible air. More likely than not, your "justlikethat" experiences were about "thinking through categories."

Let's say that you have "parakeet" as one of the birds on your list. It's very possible that the names of other birds that you know people keep as pets in their homes followed soon after your thinking of "parakeet." These would be such birds as parrot, canary, finch, minah bird—in fact, any bird you could think of that people have living with them in their homes. Some wording like "birds that people keep as pets" could be the name or label of this category (group) of birds.

But, maybe, you had "swan" on your list; you might then have thought of the category "birds that are white in color" and gone on to quickly list, "justlikethat," dove, goose, crane, and any other number of white birds. Or, still from "swan," you might have thought of the category "birds that can found in or around water," and continued right on to list duck, mallard, sea gull, and other members of the "in and around water" category of birds.

Whatever direction your mind went in, the pattern is still the same: remembering the name of just one particular kind of bird leads to your thinking about which category that particular bird belongs to or fits in, which leads to your recalling the names of several other kinds of birds in that same category.

Even better, thinking about one specific category can cause your mind to start thinking of other categories. For example, coming up with the category "birds that are white in color" might lead you, if the idea of "opposites" occurs to you, to the category "birds that are black in color." In fact, noticing the broader category of "color" could get you thinking about "birds that are especially colorful" and its opposite, "birds that are not all that colorful." These categories might then trigger—don't get dizzy, now—such additional categories as "birds where the male of the species is more colorful than the female" and "birds where the female is more colorful than the male." The process is almost endless.

What Do You Think?

Which of the experiences just described did you have as you went about compiling your list of birds?

Reflections

Consciously Categorizing

Thinking through categories, all good thinkers will tell you, works best when it is done consciously. Good thinkers make a point—and, eventually, make a practice—of actively looking for and trying out possible categories as a way to constantly improve their ability to recall information they've learned and remember "stuff" they've experienced. Good thinkers both try to generate as many categories as they can and try to generalize larger and increasingly more inclusive categories from single observations of individual and separate phenomena.

When a good thinker looks at an example of the kind of bird we call a flamingo, he or she no doubt notices that this particular type of bird has especially long legs. From that single observation, the mind of the good thinker might ask itself, "Is there a category—let me call it 'birds with long legs' that birds besides flamingos are members of, that birds like flamingos belong to?" In effect, the good thinker's mind is asking: "Are there other birds with noticeably long legs that I actually know of (through direct personal experience or from learning via various media) but that I have temporarily forgotten about (because I had no need before now to think of them)?"

As the human mind goes about forming its stockpile of categories, it is actually engaging in the process of making generalizations, the kind of thinking examined in Chapter 4 of this book. Each category label with its example is, in essence, a statement about all those things of a certain kind that we have grouped together. For instance, the category label "birds that are white in color" placed over a list that includes swans, doves, geese, and cranes is, in effect, the visualization of the generalization "Swans, doves, geese, and cranes are white-colored birds."

What Do You Think?

- list as many birds as you can think of that belong to the category "birds with long legs,"
- choose one of the long-legged birds you have included in your list and by paying attention to and singling out a different quality or feature of that long-legged bird, generate a new category of birds; give that category a meaningful name or label, and then list as many members of that new category as you can,
- practice the various "thinking through categories" techniques discussed in this chapter using at least one of the following: insects, flowers, trees,

- take one of the generalizations used as a model in Chapter 4 of this book and re-do it as a category label over a list of examples,
- take one of the category labels and lists of examples used as models in this chapter and re-do it as a generalization.

Reflections

When It's All Greek to You (Or Spanish or French)

Think back to a time when you were trying to study a foreign language (in school, in preparation for travel, for business); can you recall using a method like "thinking through categories" to memorize words you needed to or wanted to learn in that foreign language? (It doesn't matter what the language was; in fact, in could have been English, if English is not your native language.)

Often, foreign language texts introduce new vocabulary by grouping words into categories so that they can be consciously associated with one another, learned more quickly together, and retained in the learner's memory longer. Some foreign language texts go as far as to tell you that they are using the category approach (for example, "parts of the human body," or "foods," or "relationships between family members") as the organizing principle behind their presentations of word lists.

Other foreign language texts may not specifically indicate that each of their vocabulary lists centers around a particular category or mix of categories, although a quick look and some fast thinking will probably reveal this to be the case. Taking that quick look is a good idea if your future has you studying a foreign language, whatever the reason.

Mind Set

When In Rome or When It's Italian

The following list of Italian words comes from the foreign language text *Rapid Italian for Students and Tourists* by Michael Cagno and Ben D'Arlon (published by S. F. Uanni Publishers and Booksellers in 1993).

la cita—the city
la strada, la via—the street
il viale—the boulevard
il teatro—the theatre
andare a teatro—to go to the theatre
l'opera—the opera
il cinema—the movie house
il film, la pellicola—the film
il palazzo—the palace building
il treno—the train
la stazione—the station
l'automobile (fem.)—the automobile
la campagna—the country
gli alberi—the trees
alberato—tree-lined
la montagna—the mountain
l'aria—the air
il mare—the sea
il porto—the port
la spiaggia—the seashore, beach
fare i bagni—to go bathing
il costume da bagno—the bathing suit
il luogo (il luoghi)—the place

il denaro—the money

la carrozza, la vetturra—the carriage

la sorpresa—the surprise

almeno—at least

insieme—together

distrutto—destroyed

peccato!—too bad!, what a pity!

la verita—the truth

i saluti—greetings, regards

solo—alone

sicuro—sure

una volta—once

What Do You Think?

- find *at least* three categories that the words in this list could be re-arranged into, and create a label for each of the categories,
- tell how grouping certain words from the total list into your categories might help you to remember these words and their meanings,
- if you have a foreign language text handy, determine the approach it uses, chapter after chapter, in its presentation of vocabulary to be learned.

Reflections

Using Categories to Plan a Speech or Write a Report

As we have seen, creating categories is definitely not "for the birds" and can be "helpful for the words." Creating categories is a major way people give order to and organize their lives. On a less cosmic scale, creating categories can be the foundation for such key business responsibilities as writing a report or making an oral presentation in which you explain a process or procedure.

Because creating categories is at the heart of organizing facts and data, thinking through categories can be especially helpful in the business world when you need to prepare an informative report on a particular topic either for oral presentation from notes or in written form. When you prepare this kind of report, you generally need to group related facts together in different paragraphs; in other words, you need to form a category of facts per paragraph based on what the facts have in common. And what they have in common—your label for your category—can easily be turned into the sentence in each paragraph that will get across to your audience the main idea of that paragraph. Teachers of writing call the main idea in each paragraph that paragraph's topic sentence; thinking of a topic sentence as a category label written out as a full sentence will help you to do the kind of thinking known as "writing."

Mind Set

The Room You Are in Right Now

Let's say that you were asked to write a fact-based report that your audience would give you a round of applause for because it found it to be quite informative (which is the purpose of any and all informative reports). In preparation for this kind of writing, let's practice just a bit more with items that have something in common:

- look around the room you are in right now and find three items that you feel have something in common or are related in some way. Ask someone else in the room (there has to be someone else in the room, or you need to invite someone in!) to do the same thing,

- without communicating, each of you should list your three related items on a piece of paper and place a label atop the list. Be sure the label captures the nature of the category the three items belong to; for example, a chair, a bench, and a couch might be seen by one person as "pieces of furniture," by another as "objects having four legs," and by a third as "places where a person can sit."

What Do You Think?

- tell your partner what your three items are and ask your partner to guess the label you placed them under,
- have your partner tell you the three items in his or her list, and guess your partner's label,
- talk with your partner about the labels you guessed—and why they were on target, or close, or somewhat off, or way off,
- discuss with your partner why the actual labels were too easy or too hard to guess.

Mind Set

Look Again

Repeat the above Mind Set and What Do You Think?—but this time you and your partner should make a deliberate effort to find three items that are related in less obvious ways.

Mind Set

Look Again—With a Twist

Try adding more items from the room (or from outside the room) *to each other's list.*

Assessing Your Thinking

Get feedback from your partner on why each of the new items is, or is not, acceptable as a member of that category—and give your partner the same kind of feedback; in a journal entry, comment on and explain, if you can, the amount of agreement you and your partner experienced during the above process.

6

Thinking Factually Through—and Beyond— Our So-Called Right Answers

Think About It

In this chapter you will discover:

- what it most likely means when you tell someone—or someone tells you—"that's right,"
- where the line is between "fact" and "opinion" and how "thin" that line can be,
- why "factually speaking" may simply be "a difference of opinion,"
- how to think more in terms of "probability" and "possibility" and less in terms of dogmatic "certainty,"
- how rote learning and teaching to the test are not in the spirit or service of good thinking.

Mind Set

"Right You Are (If You Think You Are)"

It's a fact that . . . . I'm going to stop myself right there because, in fact, the fact is that too often in our thinking and speaking, sentences that begin with "it's a fact" end with a statement about something that might not be a fact at all—or that "all" can agree on. (Of course, that might just be my opinion!)

Similarly, the expression "right on!" may be a call for us to continue in our course of thinking—but what does it, in fact, mean when someone says we are "right" in our facts, or our ideas, or our way of thinking? (And vice versa, us to them?) Although a "right on!" affirmation has the sound of dogmatic definitiveness, more often and more likely, when someone tells us we are "right" about something, all that person is doing is letting us know that what we have thought and said *agrees* with what that person believes to be so. (And if doing this is a vice, then so is the vice versa.)

What Do You Think?

"Right You Are!"

Think back to your experiences as a student in a classroom (whatever the grade or level). Can you hear in your mind's ear, how often your teachers' voices can be heard intoning the word "right" after a question has been asked and answered? "Right!" says the teacher over and over and over again (okay, not necessarily to you!)—except when the teacher says "wrong" or "not quite."

Reflections

"Right" and "Not Quite Right"

Not quite? Flesh that phrase out and doesn't it turn into "not quite right," which is really the "short" way (both in the sense of "brief" and in the sense of "being abrupt") of a teacher's saying: "That's not quite *what I was thinking*"?

But if I say "that's not quite *what I was thinking*" to someone and it turns out that I'm wrong in my facts, or ideas, or thinking (or so I now think), then, truth be told, that other person goes in a nanosecond from being right to being wrong. Now *both of us* are wrong (in the authoritative person's opinion)—and two wrongs, well, do *they* make a "right"? (Notice my somewhat sneaky use of the word "opinion" in a paragraph purportedly dealing with a statement of "fact." Isn't that heresy? Read on.)

Mind Set

Luigi Pirandello and Alfred Hitchcock

In Italian author Luigi Pirandello's 1917 play entitled "Right You Are (If You Think You Are)," seven characters—all thoroughly middle class and with nothing but time on their hands—spend the "course" of the play arguing over their perceptions of and conclusions about a mysterious woman they can see at the window of a nearby building. You may be familiar with a similar scenario in Alfred Hitchcock's film dealing with the debatable difference between reality and the appearance of reality, "Rear Window." (And then there's the Japanese film based on the story "Rashomon," in which three men and one woman give their "take" on "what really happened" between and among them in a particular place, at a particular point in time.)

What Do You Think?

Comment on the comment "But of course there's such a thing as "certainty."

Reflections

Is It Certain That There's "Certainty"?

Pirandello's participants are passionate about their perceptions and one of Pirandello's major points in this almost plotless play is the relative nature of truth—that dogmatic *certainty* (that is, anything that smacks of the absolute, or the "purely objective," or the authoritative; or of the decisive, the conclusive, the unanimous; or of the dogma of "faith")—is impossible to come by in today's acknowledged world of relativity and consensus opinion. As children growing up, most of us were probably urged to be adult and work diligently to distinguish between fact and opinion, but in all likelihood, as we grew older, we came to realize that that was easier said than done.

Where is that clearly demarcated line where you definitely cross from one to the other? Is there a nebulous gray area that exists between the black and white of fact and opinion? Or is it absurd to talk (which is to say, to think) of even the existence of a line? This last is the question Pirandello asks—and he is but one of the more recent skeptics in what is actually a long human history of thinking about and questioning "right answers," "facts," and "reality."

Good thinkers who experience Pirandello's play "Right You Are (If You Think You Are)" must ask themselves the following fundamental question: is it probable (likely) or even possible (conceivable to the mind) for there to be complete certainty among the seven arguing characters as to the actual nature of the mysterious woman in the window?

Conspiracy theorists, it shouldn't surprise you, "trade" in this kind of questioning—and so it is instructive that William Manchester's 1967 historical account of the assassination of President John F. Kennedy (THE DEATH OF A PRESIDENT: November 22-November 25, 1963) proclaims at its start (as a kind of *caveat emptor* or "buyer beware" for its readers): "The sum of a million facts is not the truth."

Assessing Your Thinking

- consider reading, for the possible wisdom and the likely fun of it, one of the many William Shakespeare comedies that ask these questions: What is real? And what is only the appearance of reality or the semblance of reality (what only *seems* to be real)? And, ultimately, how much of what we see as real is not real *at all* but only individually or collectively illusory? For starters, how about Shakespeare's "A Mid-Summer Night's Dream"?

- or, perhaps, you could explore the less fun, but no less wise theorizing of the Greek philosopher Plato, who in a key work on the nature of reality—the one about "the myth of the cave"—hypothesized that what appeared to mankind to be real (to be reality) was simply *(simply!)* the "shadow" being cast by the "real world" just beyond mankind's vision ("vision" as in both mankind's "perception" and mankind's "imagination").

Mind Set

The Reality of "Hard Times" and of HARD TIMES

For now, let's together take a somewhat longer look at a work of literature that can serve us even better as a prototype of the rigor mortis of rote learning of facts and "right" answers; that work is the satirical novel HARD TIMES, written by the British author Charles Dickens and published, if I've got this "factually right," in 1854.

Before you react to your own assumptions and expectations of the language and characters and possible plot of an 1854 novel (don't fixate on those facts), you need to know at the start that if you find what you read in connection with HARD TIMES to be "ridiculous," you're doing some very good thinking.

And Charles Dickens would be pleased.

HARD TIMES was written as a novel of social criticism with the particular purpose of ridiculing (making fun of, holding something up to ridicule, revealing something as ridiculous because the reason it appears to be ridiculous is that it *is* ridiculous). HARD TIMES opens with a visit by Thomas Gradgrind, a fanatical "educationist" superintendent, to one of his "model" schools of the times, which Dickens is about to hold up to ridicule and scorn. Thomas Gradgrind is broadly (quite broadly) depicted by Dickens as the "murderer" of the essence of what childhood should be about—a sense of wonder and imagination.

What Do You Think?

As I've written elsewhere (my 2013 careers book *So You Think You Might Like to Teach: 23 Fictional Teachers (for Real!)*

Model How to Become and Remain a Successful Teacher), what kind of teacher supervisor would the classic British author Charles Dickens produce if that nineteenth-century master of satiric grotesquerie were to create the embodiment of *misguided* educational philosophy that valued "right" answers above all else and considered *rote learning* to be the best (and only) means to that ideal end?

- try to visualize what Mr. Gradgrind looks like—his physical attributes, his general appearance, his manner of dress, the specific "props" he would either carry or have on him, the idiosyncratic "tics" he might have, the aura he gives off,
- try to hear what Mr. Gradgrind sounds like—not only in his diction (choice of words) when he talks about his "pet" ideas but also his tone of voice and intensity of volume, any "noises" he might make, his superintendent-to-teacher conversational "style," his "teacher-to-student" conversational style,
- try, as a good thinker drawing conclusions from specific details, to infer from the very "Dickensian" name intentionally given him as much as you can about Mr. Gradgrind—both as a person and as a educational theorist,
- try to summarize any general "principles" that a Mr. Gradgrind would believe in and some particular classroom "practices" he would want to see at work in his "model" school,
- try to role-play with another person or brainstorm with a group of people the ingredients of a relatively short conversation Mr. Gradgrind and a student might have after Mr. Gradgrind has asked a "factual" question and the student has given the "wrong" answer (include any stage directions for your actors that would help to create the

atmosphere you believe would inevitably be present in this scene),

- try to predict what Mr. Gradgrind would say if asked where someone who is currently reading a book like **Good Thinking** should go to (or should do) in order to become a better thinker.

Reflections

A Look at Thomas Gradgrind (Who "Grinds" Down the Mind of Every Young Student and Any Good Thinker)

Thomas Gradgrind is "a man of realities," "a man of facts and calculations." As an educator who "proceeds upon the principle that two and two are four, and nothing over, and who is not to be talked into allowing for anything over," Thomas Gradgrind practices what he preaches. And, as a supervisor of teachers, Mr. Gradgrind "oversees" to make certain (and "certainty" is certainly one of his things) that everyone in his model school is in complete lockstep agreement with his educational philosophy.

Although teachers may not always outwardly preach their principles, what teachers believe usually underlies what they practice. Thomas Gradgrind is a triple threat: he believes, he preaches, and he practices—and the consequences of Mr. Gradgrind's misconceived philosophy of education are dire. Thomas Gradgrind is a one-man *cause-and-effect* machine.

As Dickens shows us in much detail in HARD TIMES, the result of Mr. Grandgrind's putting his philosophy into actual practice is the "murdering" of innocent young children by the *systematic* destruction of their "imaginations" and their sense of "wonder." In effect, Mr. Gradgrind's educational theory produces classroom after classroom of pupils who approach being "brain dead."

In Thomas Gradgrind's model school, good thinking is literally and figuratively unheard of because *any kind* of thinking is interrupted, condemned, and banished. Reasoning out loud by students and teachers alike is practically a sin, definitely a classroom crime, and, regrettably, a shame. (And what a shame that is!)

As Dickens summarizes it, Mr. Gradgrind fanatically believes that "the one thing needful" is that "gallons of facts"—and nothing else—be "poured" into boys and girls by their teachers. A hundred years after HARD TIMES, in the United States of America, this way of teaching and learning was sometimes referred to as "the banking model," because "deposits" of specific pieces of knowledge were repeatedly being made (through excessive lecturing and through "teaching to the test") into the minds of pupils and students. (You could "bank on it!") Still another way, in somewhat more recent times, to look as this educational "way" was the familiar metaphor (figurative comparison) of seeing a young student as "a clean slate" to be written on by the "wisdom" of the knowledgeable teacher.

But to return to the latter half of the nineteenth century, on a "fact-finding" visit to the "plain, bare, monotonous vault of a school-room" of his model primary school, Mr. Gradgrind emphatically intones his supervisory "observations" to two other individuals: the local schoolmaster and an unidentified "gentleman" visitor. Mr. Gradgrind's observations are haughty and "horticultural" in his use of the "making-a-garden-grow" metaphor: "Teach these boys and girls nothing but Facts," Mr. Gradgrind commands. "Facts alone," he continues, "are wanted in life. Plant nothing else, and root out everything else. You can only form the minds of reasoning animals upon Facts: nothing else will ever be of any service to them."

Mr. Gradgrind's misconceived educational philosophy makes educational practice imperfect; in the course of this particular supervisory visit to his "model" school, Mr. Gradgrind calls on a young girl to "define a horse." However, the child is so "thrown into the greatest alarm by this demand" that she is rendered speechless.

What Do You Think?

Did this ever happen to you in your years as a student? If so, take a few moments to think about the what, the when, and the how; then, consider the effect this terrible "teaching" had on your overall learning process

Reflections

"Possessed" (of No Facts)

Misinterpreting the female pupil's silence, an astonished Mr. Gradgrind declares her to be "possessed of no facts, in reference to one of the commonest of animals!" However, just because there is nothing coming out of this young girl's mouth does not automatically mean that there is nothing going on in her head (in her mind).

Since Thomas Gradgrind is interested *only* in regurgitated "right" answers from rote-memorized facts, his educational vision goes no further than to teach "right" from "wrong"—the "right" answer from the wrong answer; he has zero tolerance for "ignorance" and absolutely no interest in a teacher's using a wrong answer as the starting point for stimulating thinking, eliciting understanding, and, eventually, achieving actual learning. Today's "descendants" of Mr. Gradgrind all too often make the same classic classroom mistake of assuming that student silence after a teacher's question means either absence of knowledge, or lack of interest, or reluctance to reason, or inability to think. Such "anxious"—in the sense of "nervous" and not, unfortunately, in the sense of "eager"—teachers truly do not know what to make of it.

Jumping to one or more of these conclusions (and "jumping to conclusions" hardly models good thinking skills), these teachers usually solve the "problem" of silence by answering their own question or calling on the volunteer student with the "fastest hand in the class"—as though that student were a life preserver on the Titanic. Too seldom does it occur to these teachers that their silent students are actually taking the time to think through a thought-provoking question that was asked.

Instead, these modern Gradgrinds practice a kind of inquisition—clearly not an inquiry—and the sounds of their classrooms (when there is anything that breaks the silence) are the sounds of the teacher's droning voice in the mode of perpetual "oral quizzing" or of regulation #2 pencils bubbling in the practiced (over and over) so-called "right" answers to the standardized test.

Today's Gradgrinds not only never inquire into the reasoning behind a student's "wrong" answer (with a question like "What made you think that?"), they have no patience with or "tolerance" for a "wrong" answer that might actually be more insightful, more correct, more "right" (though perhaps somewhat bizarre-sounding at first) than any know-it-all teacher's established "right" answer.

Mind Set

In Conclusion (If We Have Concluded Something)— Otherwise, At the End

The title of the Pirandello play "Right You Are (If You Think You Are)" is, objectively speaking, quite subjective in its point of view; "right" (and, therefore, "wrong" as well; there's no such thing as a one-sided coin) does not exist as an unimpeachable abstract or an unassailable absolute. It's all relative: one person's well-argued (but it has to be well argued) opinion is as valid as the next person's. Reality is open to debate—which is why good thinkers strive to be open-minded, not narrow minded, not close minded.

The set of parentheses in Pirandello's title is meaningful, providing a momentary pause for on-the-spot thinking and wondering about what will come next and how it might affect the sense of the words "right you are." We've seen that "Right you are," by itself, means little more than "I agree with your opinion" (or, more accurately, "you agree with my opinion"). The addition of "if you think you are" in parentheses expresses a brand-new definition of "right" as "whatever *you* think, if *you* think it, it's so—at least for *you*." Introducing this "law" of relativity revises, in a sense, Descartes' definition of human existence ("I think; therefore, I am"). A Pirandellian definition of human existence might sound something like this: "I think I am right; therefore, I *am* right—as far as I'm concerned (and all my concerns *are* me).

Assessing Your Thinking

- comment on this statement: a "wrong" idea that might have led to a "right" idea or true "insight" may be shut off at too early a stage in a person's thinking if it cannot be justified at the moment it occurs,

- comment on this statement: there is a general assumption among people that being "right" is sufficient (adequate or enough) and that there is, therefore, no need for any additional time to be spent on thinking about the subject at hand,

- comment on this statement: in our current society, people have become afraid of sharing their thinking for fear of being branded as "wrong,"

- comment on the following excerpt from the song "Puzzlement" by Oscar Hammerstein from the 1951 Broadway musical "The King and I" in which a fictionalized king of Siam remembers that when he was a boy, the world was a better place because "what was so was so, what was not was not"; now, as a man, he finds himself questioning his formerly firm conviction that because he is in a position of authority, it follows that he is always "right":

There are times I almost think / I am not sure of what I absolutely know. / Very often find confusion / In conclusion I concluded long ago. / In my head are many facts / That, as a student, I have studied to procure, / In my head are many facts . . . / Of which I wish I was more certain I was sure! / (spoken) Is a puzzlement . . .

Shall I, then, be like my father / And be willfully unmovable and strong? / Or is it better to be right? . . . / Or am I right when I believe I may be wrong? . . .

There are times I almost think / Nobody sure of what he absolutely know. / Everybody find confusion / In conclusion he concluded long ago / And it puzzle me to learn / That tho' a man may be in doubt of what he know, / Very quickly he will fight . . . / He'll fight to prove that what he does not know is so! . . . / (spoken) But . . . is a puzzlement!

- if you think *you* might be able to think about "nothing," try it and then immediately write down what "the nothing" was that you were thinking about; be as creative as you can if you decide to tackle this task,
- there's an elephant in the room—an *actual* one, not the metaphorical one of "the big issue" people ignore, and skirt around, and don't talk about while they dither on about everything and anything (so as not to have to come to grips with a very particular "whatever"); and, forgot to mention it, this actual elephant is pink (someone painted it pink). Try to spend the next thirty seconds of your mental life not thinking of the pink elephant in the room. (Then you can think about, and talk about, or write about how well you succeeded in this task—and why you think so.)

7

Thinking Factually Through—and Out From—Our So-Called Wrong Answers, Errors, Mistakes, and Failures

Think About It

In this chapter you will discover:

- what it means when your answer is "wrong" or "you are mistaken,"
- how you can learn from "the error of your ways,"
- what it means to think "definitionally,"
- how failure can be the foundation for success,
- how cause-and-effect thinking is anything but casual.

Mind Set

Wrong You Are (If What You Think Is Not in Agreement With What Others Consider to Be "Right")

People who are inquisitive (as well as people who "profess" to be teachers) can usually be countered on to ask you all kinds of questions: often simple "yes" and "no" questions, sometimes fairly easy factual questions, and, on occasion, questions that require some heavy-duty extended analytical thinking about an established set of facts. If these people understand "the art of questioning" (questioning only becomes an "art" after you have practiced it long and hard enough as a "craft"), they can also be counted on to understand, respect, and honor "the sound of silence" on your part—the time needed by most of us, as mentioned in the preceding chapter, to think, first, about the actual meaning of the factual or reasoning-required question and, then, the time needed to process an answer and formulate a response. Unfortunately, school-based "teachers" who quickly declare "time's up" and call on the student whose hand is waving like a flag in the wind (or who answer their own question because no student has the courage to volunteer to think out loud), these "teachers" cut short—like an ax to the head—the very thinking their silent students might have been quietly engaged in.

If we could mentally eavesdrop on a good thinker's thought process, it might sound something like this: *"Huh? What did you say?"* and then *"Hmm—what is it that question is actually asking of me?"* and then *"Well, that's pretty provocative. I'm interested; you've 'got' me (I don't mean I'm stumped, I mean I'm hooked, I'm intrigued)—but do I have any thoughts on this? Well, let me think about whether I do and what they might be."*

In the case of Mr. Gradgrind, whom we met in the preceding chapter, when this "educator" does not instantaneously get what he *knows* to be the "right" answer from the young girl he called on to supply "the definition of a horse," he immediately moves on to a second non-volunteer—this time a young boy. Physically manifesting the metaphorical "squeeze" that has been put on him, this young boy literally raises the knuckles of his hands to the "freckled forehead" housing his brain and then rote-recites (without stopping for air!) what he has been repeatedly force-fed and has dutifully committed to the memory of his mind: "Quadruped. Graminivorous. Forty teeth, namely, twenty-four grinders, four eye-teeth, and twelve incisive. Sheds coat in the spring; in marshy countries, sheds hoofs, too. Hoofs hard, but requiring to be shod with iron. Age known by marks in mouth." (Large expulsion of air in relief!)

What Do You Think?

- what is your *gut reaction* to this young boy's answer?
- what do you think Mr. Gradgrind's *professional* reaction might be?
- what are your thoughts about *your* thinking, your thoughts as to why you think the way *you* do?
- how is Thomas Gradgrind a "murderer," as he's been called by Dickens, of the essence of childhood—its sense of wonder and of the imagination?
- and, oh yes, and take a deep breath and hold it: how would *you* define a horse?

Reflections

The Meanings We Make as We Make Sense of Our World

Extremely gratified by the answer he gets from the young boy, Mr. Gradgrind turns to the young girl he first called on and declares: "Now . . . you know what a horse is." Mr. Gradgrind's educational philosophy is grounded in the dual belief that the teacher is the sole source of wisdom in the classroom (the teacher as "the font" of knowledge) and that young people, *by their very nature*, would never "embrace," let alone seek out, knowledge that has not been crammed into them. (Regrettably, this philosophy is still "alive and ill" in some contemporary classrooms.)

In connection with the critical question of how knowledge is "imparted" and understanding achieved, it is essential that we consider together the role of "definitions" in the thinking processes of teaching and learning. Is the reason that definitions are "committed to memory" that they serve as observational representations of reality (of the real world as we experience it) or is it that they authoritatively prescribe what reality should be represented as—like the definition of "a horse" in HARD TIMES? In other words, should definitions make "descriptive" sense (telling it as observationally and operationally as possible, verbally capturing what something appears to be or how it appears to "work") or should definitions make "prescriptive" sense (telling it like someone with linguistic authority says it "is" or should be)?

Truly good thinking about any area of knowledge can only be done using the actual *content* of that body of knowledge. When human beings think, they think about "something"—some "thing." Thinkers need to know the facts—and know how to make use of them—when engaged in even the lowest level of the thinking process (we're not talking here, not yet, about higher level critical thinking or creative thinking). No one can be thinking about "nothing" (no "thing")—although that is sometimes what young people say they are thinking about when directly asked by an adult (usually a parent), "What are you thinking?" ("Nothing, dad"; "nothing, mom.")

Higher level critical thinking and creative thinking (now we're talking!) is no different from lower levels of thinking in that they must be about something: about a body of knowledge, about a family of facts. All thinking starts with particular observations (and sometimes, unfortunately, a mistaken set of assumptions about those facts), then tries to make connections among these specific details, then looks to discover patterns across the connections, and then, tentatively, makes inferences and draws conclusions from and about these patterns (subject to change in the course of time without notice—but, also, subject to change when additional "noticing" occurs).

It would seem, then, that what is essential about any body of knowledge, about any content is that its definitions be as concrete, specific, particular, visual, functional, and definitionally operational (phrased in terms of not what something "is" but in terms of how that something "operates") as possible. In short, the definitions you use in your thinking, your speaking, your writing (in your work, in your play, in your life) should be more descriptive than prescriptive.

As the medically trained novelist Blake Charlton wrote in May of 2013, in a "New York Times" op-ed opinion piece about thinking definitionally about medical diagnoses:

> Before I went to medical school, I thought a diagnosis was synonymous with a fact; criteria were met, or not. Sometimes this is so. Diabetes, for example, can be determined with a few laboratory tests.

> But other diagnoses, particularly those involving the mind, are more nebulous. Symptoms are contradictory, test results equivocal. Moreover, the definition of almost any diagnosis changes as science and society evolve.

Diagnostics may have more in common with law than science. Legislatures of disease exist in expert panels, practice guidelines and consensus papers. Some laws are unimpeachable, while others may be inaccurate or prejudiced. The same is true of medicine; consider the antiquated diagnosis of hysteria in women. Those affected by unjust diagnoses—like those affected by unjust laws—should protest and help redefine them.

What Do You Think?

- do Charlton's thoughts constitute nothing more than one doctor's opinion of what the facts are when it comes to medical diagnoses and the wording of their definitions? Explain why you think so, or not,
- think about Charlton's thinking—because *he* does and then he proceeds to engage in the kind of thinking known as thinking through an *analogy*, in this particular case making an analogy between the field of medicine (particularly "mental" medicine) and the field of science and the field of law (and finding medicine and the law to be similar),
- if you're curious—and good thinkers generally are—research the antiquated diagnosis and the modern (that is, *current*) diagnosis of hysteria.

Reflections

Really?

Because legal and medical definitions (and most other "high-toned" definitions) come across as, well, "definitive," good thinkers should examine these definitions carefully before making them the basis of their considered opinions and points of view.

As a "rule" (careful, now) of thumb, it is probably most often the case that the more prescriptive the definition, the more precarious the "position." My use of "probably" in the preceding sentence purposely makes the point that caution is strongly advised when an individual's first thought is a word or phrase like "certainly" or "absolutely" or "surely" or "apparently" or "of course." Such definitiveness can sometimes leave that individual without a leg to stand on—and good thinkers on the receiving end of such "certainty" might be wise to respond with "Really?" For real.

On the other hand (and we're thinking out loud here), if something is logically "conceivable," then it is "possible"—and if it is possible, then it can be looked into and a determination can be made as to, as to what? *As to* whether we can go as far as to say (and to think, which should ideally precede our saying) that it is "probable." Really? Really! Make no mistake about it!

Oops, make fewer mistakes about it—and work to learn, repeatedly, from those mistakes, for it is from our mistakes and errors and failures (if we are unembarrassedly open-minded about ourselves and open enough to the whole "trial and error" thing) that we do our most productive learning. Our so-called successes, on the other other hand, may fail to teach us all that much because we tend to see our own personal successes as "sufficient unto themselves."

Why? Because they were sufficient or adequate or good-enough as solutions to the problem at hand. What's more to think about? Well, here's what: *why* it worked—so that you understand how to make it work that same way again for another problem you might face someday. (This insight should remind you of what was said earlier about how thinking about the process that led up—or down—to a "wrong" answer can be mindfully more valuable than happily coming up with the "right" answer.)

Sometimes the error in our thinking is the result of confusing "time sequence" with "cause and effect." One fairly easy way to cut down on the number of times you make this mistake is simply to make a conscious point of trying to remember that just because one thing comes after another doesn't mean that the first thing caused the second thing to happen. It might help to think of this mistake in cause-and-effect thinking as the difference between the word "causal" and the word "casual."

What Do You Think?

Do you think you just read the same word twice and are confused about why the sentence is talking about "difference"?

Reflections

Causal Isn't Casual

Look again at the two words: causal / casual. In the first, the "u" comes before the "s" because (as in "because") the word is all about how one thing that has happened *causes* something else to happen afterwards.

However, in "casual," the "u" comes after the "s" and the word is all about "informal" or "relaxed" or "not seriously connected," as in "the two co-workers were not close; they had a casual relationship" (they were little more than acquaintances). When one thing happens and then another thing happens right after it or a little bit later in time, that sequence *didn't necessarily have to be*; the relationship in time is informal, "casual," not "causal"—unless there is the *additional and essential* factor of the second thing's being the result of the first. ("You made me love you; I didn't want to do it, I didn't want to do it" is a classic song lyric that for me captures the inevitability of every cause-and-effect relationship.)

So, good thinkers are always careful to examine the nature of the relationship between two things that appear in some kind of sequence. Just because one thing "followed hard upon" another (Prince Hamlet's disapproving reference to his mother's marrying her late husband's brother soon after her husband's funeral) does not necessarily mean that the second thing "had to follow" the first, that it was caused by it (that it was the effect or result of the initial impetus).

And while we are on the subject of errors in our thinking about a "sequence" of events, it is time to re-write the saying that "nothing succeeds like success" (remembering that one meaning of "to succeed" is "to come after or to follow directly upon in a sequence" or succession). Better to start quoting "nothing succeeds like failure" since more often than we care to acknowledge, it is only after repeated failures that most of us learn how to truly "succeed." Isn't this the philosophy behind the admonition to "try, try again" if at first you don't succeed?

Mind Set

In Conclusion

As we come to the close of this relatively short chapter, we should not reach it without saying a few words about the difference in the English language between thinking of someone as "ignorant" and thinking of someone as "stupid." This difference hinges on the fact that the word "ignorant" is related to the word "ignore"; thus it might be said that people who are not mentally "deficient" (not "stupid") but who are "ignorant" about something (have "no knowledge" of that something's existence) are ignorant because they have been "ignoring" a particular set of actual things until now.

But "now," the moment has arrived to acknowledge those particular facts, and having ac**knowledge**d them, these people are, now, not only **knowledge**able but will, in the future, recognize them ("re**cog**nize" literally means they will "know again" the next time they come upon them). Did you **know** *that* from the root or stem "cog" and the prefix "re"?

However, it is possible that these ignorant people may have also been "stupid" all along because they were not intelligent enough (mentally "sufficient") to work on their ignorance problem for all those years.

Assessing Your Thinking

- so far, in this book, the kind of thinking we've been thinking about has, in the past, been referred to by some good thinkers as "vertical thinking"; draw a ladder and then use what your ladder looks like to come up with a possible explanation of what "vertical thinking" specifically consists of,
- write in your personal journal as complete and detailed and operational a definition of what "vertical thinking" is "all about."

8

Thinking Laterally (Outside the Box)

Think About It

In this chapter you will discover:

- how to "fix" your fixated assumptive thinking,
- how to think laterally (outside the box) and, possibly, more creatively,
- how to use brainstorming in the service of lateral thinking.

Mind Set

See That Box? Are You Thinking Inside It or Outside It?

You may have heard people talk about the creative importance of knowing how to think "outside the box," but don't do any thinking about that quite yet; instead, draw a picture of what you think "inside-the-box" thinking looks like or consists of; in other words (actually, in no words!), *visualize* through a sketch "inside-the-box" thinking. (No reading any further until you do. Please.)

What Do You Think?

- now that you've finished your sketch, explain, verbally, why you drew the picture the way you did (you started visual, now go verbal),
- next, draw the "opposite" picture of the picture you just drew so that you wind up with what you think "outside-the-box" thinking looks like or consists of; picture this: again you are starting with the visual,
- finally (you can predict what's coming, right?—predicting is a very high level critical thinking skill), explain, verbally, why you drew the picture the way you did,
- tell why you would rather be breathing inside a box or outside a box.

Reflections

Lateral Thinking (It's Outside-the-Box Thinking)

All this talk about boxes—and then breathing!—can't help but put you in mind of the particular box many people whose mortal lives are over end up spending eternity in. That was intentional on my part—admittedly morbid, but intentional (I have my reasons). One other thing we would probably agree on is that human beings would rather do their breathing *outside* rather than inside the confines of a box (no matter how much air there is in that box to start with!).

If you are feeling restrained or confined right now, you are exactly where you need to be to understand why people talk so much these days about "outside-the-box" thinking. If you start with a mental image of conventional thinking as the kind of thinking being done if we were somehow "within" the enclosed four sides of a two-dimensional box, then breaking out past the perimeter of that box becomes the image for thinking in a freer, the-sky's-the-limit way.

Consequently, outside-the-box thinking is considered by many (particularly in the business world) to be one of the major ways you can be more creative in your thinking. The often off-beat conclusions resulting from outside-the-box thinking (previously unheard of ideas, insights, and solutions) can initially be controversial because, no question about it, they challenge "the current thinking" by going beyond the obvious and accustomed habits of reasoning, by discarding preconceived notions and unexamined assumptions, and by viewing problems from unexpected perspectives.

In a June of 2013 article in "The New York Times" on the passing of Nobel-prize-winning economist and University of Chicago professor Robert W. Fogel, a former student of his commented: "Everything Bob touches is controversial; it stems from the fact that he thinks outside the box."

Here's an example from early in Professor Fogel's career: based on his research, in 1964 Professor Fogel challenged the accepted thinking that it was the emergence of the railroads in American history that was *the* key factor in the country's economic growth. Professor Fogel maintained that the railroads had been "far less important to the nation's growth than economists had long asserted . . . that wheat, corn, pork and beef—the four major agricultural goods—would have been shipped on existing water routes and by wagon had railroads not been available."

Who would have thought!

Who would have thought? Well, thinkers who think both laterally and vertically would have thought.

Lateral thinking? *Vertical* thinking?

What Do You Think?

Return, for a moment, to the thinking and drawing you did in the Assessing Your Thinking section at the end of the last chapter; review (re-view) your work.

Reflections

Climbing the Ladder to Success

Thinking pictorially (and metaphorically), it's not too difficult to see a similarity between a person's ascending a well-constructed ladder—step by steady step to the ladder's uppermost level—and the kind of determined sequential thinking that can eventually lead to a satisfactory conclusion.

Such ladder-like *vertical thinking* is the kind of thinking that, generally speaking, most good thinkers engage in and succeed at; in other words, it's the kind of conventional and traditional thinking described, exemplified, and practiced throughout much of this book. To give vertical thinking a more formal definition, we could say that it involves: an individual thinker's starting from a comfortable context (or frame of reference or set of working assumptions) and proceeding forward (or upward) in sequential steps (where each step needs to be analytically justified before the person moves on to the next).

What matters most in vertical thinking is "rightness," the kind of "being right" in your answers that we examined in the previous chapter. When you are engaged in vertical thinking, you may start by looking for a whole bunch of different approaches to a problem or puzzling situation, but you must then select what you consider to be the best possible or most promising approach, discard the others, and, confident that you are on the right path, proceed "right on!"

What Do You Think?

Make a quick sketch that you could then label "lateral thinking," knowing that "lateral" means "sideways."

Mind Set

Lateral Thinking

Lateral thinking, on the other hand (the left hand—the hand "left" over after you push the "right" hand aside), strives to open up a multitude of approaches, resisting the very human temptation to evaluate and judge each and every approach as it comes to mind and to reject as many as possible as "wrong." Lateral thinking works to expand the pool of conceivable approaches, answers, and solutions, whereas vertical thinking is always working to narrow the pool, eliminating any and all that don't appear, at the moment, to be "it."

In fact, lateral thinking has at its goal the *generation* of as many "answers" as possible *for the sake of generating as many answers as possible*. (The technique of brainstorming—an aid to the good thinking to be achieved by a *group* of people—may be the implementation of lateral thinking most familiar to most of you; more about "brainstorming" later in this chapter.)

Since the very name "lateral thinking" suggests a moving sideways or "this way and that" instead of moving straight ahead on an already chosen or determined path, we might make the analogy that: lateral thinking is to vertical thinking as the actual trying of a whole bunch of unconnected detours is to the faithful following of a location and mileage printout from MapQuest.

In vertical thinking, there is movement forward only if "a next step" can be envisioned, examined, and executed, with each sequential step arising out of but still logically connected to the preceding one. Once a single conclusion is reached by a person engaged in vertical thinking (and conclusions are never "jumped to" because that would skip or eliminate necessary steps), the soundness of that conclusion rests on the soundness of the steps leading directly up to it. In a sense, you have arrived home and the key fits in the lock and opens the door. (Traditional logical thinking, including mathematical thinking, is dependent upon this.)

In lateral thinking, all movement is self-directed, coming solely from your desire to generate another and another and another *alternative direction* to go in before any actual direction is ultimately selected. Because in lateral thinking the "steps" do not have to be either sequential or resulting from any preceding ones, you can "jump ahead" (there really is no "ahead"), and skip around, and then go "back." In lateral thinking when you happen to jump to what you believe is "the" conclusion, it is "right" because it makes sense to you without being dependent on the process that got you there. In fact, in true outside-the-box thinking, you know from the start that there is actually no box there at all. For example, in the process known as "trial-and-error," a successful trial is still successful even if there was no good reason for trying it; similarly, in lateral (outside-the-box) thinking, if you have a "hunch," you of course "go for it."

What Do You Think?

- this is a "yes" or "no" question about what you think you understand at this point in the chapter about lateral thinking: with lateral thinking, does the thinker continue to generate more and different approaches after an approach that has already been generated seems "promising"?
- tell why you answered the way you did.

Reflections

Generating Additional Directions

Because in vertical thinking you move along a determined path toward a solution to a problem, the "correct" answer to the What Do You Think? question is "yes"; in lateral thinking, you move for the sake of moving—and you don't have to be moving towards something; you can be moving away from something. The purpose of lateral thinking is not to move in a particular direction but to generate more possible directions. Or as was said by the British psychologist Edward de Bono in one of his best-known works on outside-the-box thinking, the 1970 book LATERAL THINKING:

> It is the movement or change that matters . . . ; with lateral thinking, one designs an experiment in order to provide an opportunity to change one's ideas . . . ; with lateral thinking one may play around without any purpose or direction.

In short, to again quote de Bono, The vertical thinker says: "I know what I am looking for." The lateral thinker says: "I am looking but I won't know what I am looking for until I have found it." And de Bono one more time: "You cannot dig a hole in a different place by digging the same hole deeper."

Clearly, if they are thinking laterally, good thinkers never abruptly respond to an idea that suddenly occurs to them with the immediate self-rejecting shutdown of a "no." In fact, sometimes it is absolutely necessary that a thinker's idea be actually *seen by others* to be "oh-so-obviously wrong" (in the classroom, on the job, in life) in order for the thinker to turn out to be "right" in the end. And it is only the end that matters, not the configuration of the "means" by which the end was ultimately reached. This is also why "backwards" thinking is very much a part of thinking laterally because, as de Bono puts it: "It may be necessary to be on the top of a mountain in order to find the best way up."

What Do You Think?

What would you say to someone who tells you that something you've just said (as an expression of your thinking) is "irrelevant" or "beside the point"? Why would you give that response?

Reflections

Fixing Your Fixated Thinking

Is it evident by now that when someone is looking for only those ideas, responses, words, images, and so on that are "relevant," that person is well ensconced inside the box of inside-the-box thinking and is not interested in breaking any of the conventional patterns. As we discovered in an early chapter of this book, when we are thinking vertically we are always putting things into the box, identifying them and labeling or naming them as part of an ordered and fixed group or category. Since vertical thinking largely works by breaking things down into their already component parts and taking a good hard evaluative and judgmental look at each part in succession (in other words, by *analyzing*), it stands to reason that this "fixation" will narrow the likelihood of a freer and more creative thinking—one, like lateral thinking, that *starts* with the actual *generating* of the "parts" for later possible *synthesizing* (a bringing and putting together) into previously unthought of solutions, solutions that will not fit into the "pigeonhole" of rigid, authoritative definition and conventional classification.

What Do You Think?

Do you feel that you are capable of—or comfortable with—more lateral thinking in your life? Use vertical thinking to analyze your response.

Reflections

Completing Yourself With Lateral Thinking

Lateral thinking can never substitute for the vertical, more analytical thinking that we do day in and day out (nor should it); both vertical and lateral thinking are necessary for a fuller thoughtful and mindful life. Each type of thinking complements (completes) the other.

And truth be told, not all of us can be all "that" creative. But does each of us truly know just how big that "that" is? If we fail to make room in our vertical thinking for the complementary thinking of lateral thinking, we rob ourselves of the greater freedom to think more creatively, because with lateral thinking, labels and categories change and fixations go fluid when we look at things in a new way.

Creative thinkers are those individuals who go off in the least obvious directions, not the most likely ones. "Who knows where this may lead?" is the kind of "signpost" creative thinkers pay particular attention to. While vertical thinking offers the expectation of an answer or a solution—perhaps only a minimally satisfactory solution, but, still, *a solution*—lateral thinking, while increasing the *chances* for true insight or maximum resolution, offers no guarantees. The only thing that can be said, with certainty, about thinking laterally, is that it is ripe with possibility.

Mind Set

Pippin and Us

In the 1972 Broadway musical "Pippin," music and lyrics by Stephen Schwartz, the audience is invited to "join us" and go along as spectators to the life journey of Pippin, the adolescent son of the great emperor Charlemagne; standing in his father's huge shadow, Pippin wants to be the "hero" of his own life and believes that the only way to achieve that goal is to make something really quite special of himself or to do something utterly "extraordinary" (way beyond "ordinary"—literally, extra ordinary).

What Do You Think?

But What Do You Think Being Extraordinary Involves, Pippin?

What are some of the possible ways that a young man (or woman) can "dream of" and "dream up" to find his or her own "corner of the sky" (as a key song lyric of Pippin's puts it)?

Reflections

Climbing a Ladder to Success

An actual ladder is prominently used in the 2013 Broadway revival of "Pippin" to symbolize the vertical thinking that it is assumed will lead its title character to what other characters in the story already consider Pippin's destiny or fate—in other words, the answer to the perennial human question "Who am I?" However, lateral thinking enters the picture quite late in the show in the form of a young widow and her son who, well, provide the first outside-the-box possible solution to Pippin's step-by-logical-step approach to his life's problem. I won't spoil the selection of Pippin's "heroic" life choice for you, but you might like to *predict* what you think it is and then check it out by either seeing a production of the show or researching the show in print or online.

Assessing Your Thinking

Explain where and why each of the following can be considered an example of vertical thinking and lateral thinking complementing each other:

- a fireman is conventionally defined as an individual officially trained and employed to control and put out fires that have been accidentally or purposely set. In the American writer Ray Bradbury's futuristic novel FAHRENHEIT 451, a 1953 novel that deals with a totalitarian state vigilant in its obliteration of rebellious ideas, the governmental job of "fireman," however, means and involves something else. Tell what it is you think the "firemen" of this society are hired to do, and then think about your thinking: where did you use vertical thinking, and how do you know that? Where did you use lateral thinking, and how do you know that? Talk about this out loud to yourself or in your personal journal,

- make a deliberate effort to think outside the box in order to more readily come up with answers to the following riddle-type questions found in online searches under "lateral thinking" (as a spur to your creative thinking, a reminder that "lateral" refers to "side"):

  o   what can you put in a wooden box that would make it lighter (the more of them you put in, the lighter the box becomes, yet the box remains empty)? Huh?
  o   which side of a cat contains the most hair? Hmm.
  o   a window cleaner is cleaning the windows on the 37th floor of a skyscraper when he slips and falls; he is not wearing a safety harness and nothing slows his fall, yet he suffers no injuries. Huh?

- HELP ELEANOR COME HOME
  these four words mysteriously appear one day on a wall of a house known as Hill House (up on a hill, or named after the Hill family, or . . . ? I'm just thinking out loud here; and I'm not telling, only warning you not to make any assumptions). Hill House does exist, however; it exists fictionally in a quite famous novel, THE HAUNTING OF

HILL HOUSE, by American author Shirley Jackson (yes, the same Shirley Jackson who wrote the short story "After You, My Dear Alphonse"). Before reading any further, write down in you own words what you think these four words are saying *to you* despite their lack of punctuation. ***Then read this***: Eleanor is a high-anxiety unmarried woman of a certain age who has agreed to journey from her own home where she lives alone (and where, for many years, she had taken care of her now-deceased mother); she will temporarily join several others at Hill House who received similar invitations; all have been summoned by a psychiatrist to participate in a scientific experiment within and about the house (which may or may not be haunted): using lateral thinking (which is to say, be creative, not conventional), punctuate (with periods, commas, semi-colons, exclamation marks, colons, question marks, whatever) these words that appear on the wall so that the sentence or sentences that you create in each case come to make a different sense (have a different meaning) every time you play around with the punctuation. You may NOT change the order of the four words, eliminate any of them, or substitute or add new words. Create as many different meanings (make as much sense) as you can, being sure to give yourself plenty of time to break through the perimeter of any box you think you see before you.

Mind Set

Brainstorming

Just as baseball is a sport played by a team in a formal stadium built for that purpose, the team activity known as brainstorming ("storming" the brain) is itself *the formal setting* for lateral thinking engaged in by a group. In brainstorming sessions, the non-stop ideas "spit out" loud enough to be heard by all are meant to be provocative; literally, their very purpose is to "provoke" (to stimulate) more ideas from everyone else. Within the creativity of lateral thinking, brainstorming is the equivalent of having a heavy rainstorm of other people's ideas both lay siege to and unearth the ideas that had taken root and were slowly growing in your mind.

If a properly done brainstorming session were to be audiotaped, there would be nothing on the tape that sounded at all like someone's evaluation or judgment of anything anyone else had just (or had earlier) said. In fact, even if an individual's spoken idea was misunderstood by some members of the group, that no-negative-feedback-allowed misunderstanding would not be questioned and might very well wind up being the "storm" or stimulus to another person's thinking. (Speaking of tape-recording, that is one of the ways that the ideas in a brainstorming session get noted for the record if they are not handwritten down or imputed on an electronic device for group sharing at a later time.)

Most important of all, because there is no time or space for criticism, censure, approval, rejection, immediate acceptance (you get the idea), it is not uncommon that an idea that might have struck someone as obvious (or bizarre, or trivial) in a non–brainstorming context is freed up to bang up against and combine with the ideas of other members of the group and produce major insights, original conclusions, or creative solutions. With judgment of ideas suspended, people who normally fear being laughed at for their thinking soon learn to become comfortable in a quite formal setting in which they can offer up ideas that may be old, may be new, may even be borrowed, or could possibly be "blue."

As the American composer and lyricist Cole Porter wrote, "anything goes" in brainstorming sessions: no idea can be subjected to ridicule—and so nothing ever said can be considered "ridiculous." (To nip an evaluation in the bud, a chairman of the brainstorming session needs to be chosen and present to interrupt and say something like, "uh, uh, that's evaluation; now stop it!" or "it doesn't matter that that idea's been tried elsewhere; let's have your idea and talk about it later.")

What Do You Think?

Consideration of a brainstorming session's ideas will normally take place in a follow-up evaluation session with either the original group or another group of people doing the judging. If you were in charge of such an evaluation group, how would you recommend categorizing and labeling (for use and reference) the ideas under consideration?

Reflections

What to Do After the Brainstorm Has Abated

It is, of course, in the evaluation session that the kind of thinking known as critical analysis comes prominently into play. Needless to say, without such an analytical follow-through, formal brainstorming loses its major reason for being, which is to produce a wealth of ideas to compare and contrast, evaluate and judge, keep and discard. In general, three categories of retain-for-the-time-being ideas result from an evaluation session: (1) proposals of immediate practical use; (2) innovative approaches to the central problem that served as the catalyst for the original brainstorming session; and (3) areas worthy of future or further reference and exploration.

Mind Set

In Conclusion

As I pointed out in the last chapter (in English, when someone says that *another someone* "pointed out" something, it always seems to mean that the second person *totally agrees* with what the first person made a point of saying) . . . . Let me start again, as we have seen (uh, oh, I'm assuming your complete agreement), being stupid and being ignorant are not at all the same thing, but they may co-habitate in the same person's mind. It would seem that you can have a "world of knowledge" within you (so you're *far* from "ignorant") but you can still be *near* "stupid." And if you're more than a little "stupid," you're probably not smart enough to recognize the value of not ignoring things.

As to the differences between vertical thinking and lateral thinking, although the processes are quite different and distinct, both are necessary in the fuller life of a good thinker. It is not only that these two kinds of thinking complement each other but also that when it appears to you that you are completely lost in your everyday vertical thinking, there is nothing to be lost by moving on to thinking laterally. Lateral thinking always holds out the possibility that when you are faced with a blank wall, you may very possibly come up with a way around or through that wall.

Assessing Your Thinking

How wise (or otherwise) do you find the following? How come?

- the truly wise person is the person who "knows not and knows that he knows not,"

- the fool is a person who "knows not and knows not that he knows not,"
- we learn not from our successes but from our errors, mistakes, and failures,
- it's ridiculous (deserving of ridicule) to expect a different result from repeating again and again the same unsuccessful procedure,
- no teacher of any subject can effectively teach that subject without simultaneously teaching students how to think critically using the subject's specific content. Evidence, data, facts—these raw materials are necessary for true thinking and real understanding of any particular anything. Raw materials by their very nature are always descriptive, never prescriptive. Therefore (the argument goes), the more descriptive the definitions of a field of study's key terms, the more likely it is that students will remember and comprehend the significance of the raw material they are being asked to analyze, synthesize, and draw inferences from.

9

Thinking Visually Through "Picture This!"

Think About It

In this chapter you will discover that "thinking pictorially" through things like *graphs* and *charts* is one of several types of *non-verbal* thinking (thinking that bypasses the use of words)—and since this is a book exclusively about *verbal* thinking, that other kind of thinking is meant for another book (perhaps by another author).

Good Thinking is purposely and purposefully a self-improvement approach to the most important forms of *verbal thinking* we human beings engage in. So thinking pictorially, I am, good reader, almost literally out of words.

Except to tell you that most of the "good thinking" that we do and that is dealt with in all the other chapters of this book involves a high degree of mental and mindful visualization. One of the things, for example, that makes good readers good readers is that they have worked on developing their ability to visualize—to create mental pictures as they read. Such visualization is a key not only to comprehending what you are reading as you are reading and thinking about it but also to retaining that understanding in your memory for future reference. Not so incidentally, for a currently and readily available reference that combines verbalization (word choice) and planned visualization (design), see the front cover of this book, **Good Thinking**: check out such purposeful elements as the use of thought "balloons," the look of the layout, the selection of four different colors (why the predominant shade of green?), the degree of brightness of tone, the variety of fonts. Think about how well, or not, the individual verbalizations and visualizations work together to communicate their respective feelings and ideas and create an overall impact; then, think about your thinking and what produced these ideas in your mind.

And now, a quick preview of the next chapter, which is on "thinking metaphorically"—not incidentally, a major example of thinking visually—of telling the mind to "picture this!"

Mind Set

Now, the end of this chapter—and the beginning of the next.

10

Thinking Metaphorically
(Whenever You Have a Flight of Fancy)

Think About It

In this chapter—which is more than a page or so long, I promise—you will discover:

- how to understand what a metaphor "is" and what a metaphor "does"; in short, how to "nail" the concept of metaphor,
- how to appreciate what metaphors are for,
- how to be aware when and why you—and others—use metaphor after metaphor after metaphor like "a running faucet,"
- how to know when to put "the brakes" on your metaphors, especially if you are mixing the ones that you make,
- how to avoid ("like the plague!") metaphors that are clichés.

Mind Set

Swinging for the Fences, Metaphorically Speaking

Let's start this regular-length chapter on thinking "through metaphors" by hitting you over the head the way a hammer repeatedly goes for the head of a nail (yes, that's a metaphor):

In a 2012 "New York Times" film review by the critic A. O. Scott (of the movie "Trouble With the Curve"), Scott summarizes the movie as being *about* a man by the name of Gus Lobel, a longtime scout for the Atlanta Braves baseball team (played by Clint Eastwood, who also directed the film) whose eyesight is failing and whose job is threatened by a younger man.

However, in commenting on the "expert" and "satisfying" performance in the film by the actress Amy Adams, film critic Scott remarks that Mr. Eastwood "has the good sense to realize that, much as we may adore him, we'd sometimes rather spend time with Ms. Adams, who somehow grows tougher, funnier, scarier and more charming with every role."

Then Mr. Scott adds in his review that the film "may be an exhibition game, with nothing much at stake, but Ms. Adams brings the heat. She swings for the fence. Snags the line drive, tags the runner and makes the throw to the plate. Find your own metaphor."

Before you "find your own metaphor" (ideally by experiencing Ms. Adams's performance for yourself), you should be able right now to find all of Mr. Scott's metaphors, even though you may not be all that clear as to what a metaphor is or does. Mr.

Scott helpfully implies that he has provided a few metaphors of his own so all you have to do is look back on the type of imaginative language he made use of to praise Ms. Adams's performance and try to discover a pattern to Mr. Scott's phrases that gets across his enthusiasm for what he might otherwise have called a performance that was quite expert, or truly terrific, or the best.

Not only was each of Mr. Scott's pieces of praise the figure of speech (more accurately, the configuration of language) we call a metaphor but because they were all metaphors from the very same content source—the world of baseball—Mr. Scott has actually hit, metaphorically speaking, "a home run" in the form of an *extended* metaphor.

So, already without our providing a dictionary-type definition of what a metaphor *is*, you have a beginning sense of what a metaphor *does* (and descriptive definitions, you may recall from another chapter, are *operational* definitions: things "are" what they "do"). You can prove this new understanding to yourself right now by taking the time—before you read any further—to either say out loud everything you think you know about metaphors or you can write down everything you think you have just figured out about how metaphors operate. Then read on—because I have a story to tell you. (You have may noticed—I'm hoping so—that from time to time in this book one of the ways used to instruct or teach about good thinking is for me to tell a story, or an anecdote, or a joke about something from which a key point about thinking can reasonably be concluded or inferred; "thinking through and concluding from anecdotes" is a powerful way of becoming a better thinker.)

Anyway, as I was about to say: The story is told of the man who one day was informed (as in given some information new to him) that even though he might not know what a metaphor was, he had often been overheard talking in them. (Big Brother was listening!) Scared sh-tless, the man (it could also be a woman) asked if there was anything that could be done to cure him (her) of this condition before the world caught wind of it.

As if this story wasn't as unsettling as a bull in a china shop, there soon followed other stories of other men and women who, when told that they were constantly using metaphors when they spoke, couldn't accept that assertion because they had been accustomed to believe—like members of a naive cult—that only the most sophisticated of people could manage a metaphor; mere peasants couldn't possibly have the necessary tools!

So, not only "what is a metaphor *for*?" but also "*who* is a metaphor for?"

What Do You Think?

- how does the use of the visually imaginative metaphor "as unsettling as a bull in a china shop" in one of the paragraphs above NOT *mix* well with some of the other metaphors that appear in an earlier paragraph? (Good thinkers tend to frown on the use of *mixed metaphors* in spoken and written English.),
- which of the following expresses the stronger feeling of dislike? (a) I dislike broccoli, (b) I prefer spinach to broccoli but, truth be told, I don't care that much for spinach, either, (c) I really dislike broccoli, (d) I really, really dislike broccoli, (e) I just can't begin to tell you how much I dislike broccoli.

Reflections

When You Have a Choice of
Which Vegetables Not to Eat First

If you answered either (a), (b), or (c), what were you thinking? Doesn't the repetition of "really" in choice (d) trump the single "really" in choice (c)? One of the major jobs of repetition in spoken and written language—which is to say in the thinking that we do—is to call attention to something (to focus in on it) by saying it again (and, perhaps, again—just in case the hearer or reader hadn't paid sufficient attention to it in the first place).

And, doesn't the single "really" in choice (c) not only trump choice (a)'s no "really" at all but also trump choice (b), the mealy-mouthed "dislike comparison" of "I prefer spinach to broccoli, but, truth be told, I don't care that much for spinach, either"?

And, to think again, doesn't the exhausted reluctance and implied magnitude of the job to be done of "I just can't begin to tell you how much I dislike broccoli" trump any number of ordinary repetitions of "really"? I mean, really? As in, come on, what were you thinking?

So, if I am right about this (which means I think that I've got you to finally agree with me)—and even if you may feel you have a strong argument to make in favor of choice (d) over choice (e), the wording of choice (e), although never making use of a metaphor, does give a solid hint as to why whenever people think, and speak, and write, they wind up reaching for metaphors and other ways to "grow" language—whether they realize it or not.

Metaphors are born out of frustration—the frustration inherent in using, time and again, and again, ineffective ordinary language. Feel that frustration now by trying to convey how much you truly dislike broccoli through using a word like "really" or "very" or "extremely" once or twice or "x" number of times.

So the question a good thinker asks is: how can I really, really, really get across my dislike of broccoli without using "really" even once (because so many people—too many—use "really" so often that the listener to or reader of that act of communication doesn't even hear it or see it)?

Choice (e), then, is an attempt to deal with this pervasive problem of common communication by making use of an original COMPARISON, or a perceptive EXAGGERATION, or a noticeable INTENSITY. It's as if you were speaking in upper case (those capital letters are metaphorical) in order to come across in a less usual, less familiar way—TO STAND UP AND TO STAND OUT. And that's what a metaphor is, and that's what a metaphor does, and that's what a metaphor is for. And that's why a metaphor works (when it works).

TO STAND OUT. TO CALL ATTENTION TO. TO ASK TO BE NOTICED. SO AS TO BE HEARD. SO AS TO BE REALLY, REALLY, REALLY UNDERSTOOD.

So the question a good thinker asks is: how does a metaphor do this? Glad you asked, and as a working example of a metaphor from a recent piece of literature, here's how American author Dennis Lehane, in his 2012 novel LIVE BY NIGHT, talks about something metaphorically (you'll not have too much trouble finding it because metaphors stand up and out if you're looking for them or listening for them; you'll, of course, want to state what that "something" is, and you can do that by filling in the blank after "very, very" _____ once you've visualized the metaphor):

> South Station was a transfer station where three subway lines, two el lines, a streetcar line, two bus lines, and the commuter rail all converged. Stepping out of the car and onto the platform turned him into a billiards ball on the break—he was bounced, pinned, and bounced again.

Assessing Your Thinking

Go back to the opening Mind Set of this chapter; re-read it with the purpose in mind of locating instances of "metaphor" based on your new (tentative) understanding of what a metaphor is, what a metaphor does, what a metaphor is for, and why a metaphor works. (No need to look up what a standard dictionary has to saying about the "meaning" of metaphor; in fact, resist the temptation for now.)

List the metaphors you find and explain (in a journal entry or out loud to yourself) how, and how well, these possible metaphors work to achieve the effect they strive for: to overcome—for the sake of more effective communication—the weaknesses of more ordinary, more familiar, more common language.

What Do You Think?

Does your list of possible metaphors include at least some of the following examples? Do your explanations resemble those given for the examples below?

- (a) "Big Brother was listening!"
- (b) "Scared sh-tless,"
- (c) "to cure him of this condition,"
- (d) "before the world caught wind of it,"
- (e) "like members of a cult,"
- (f) "manage a metaphor,"
- (g) "mere peasants,"
- (h) "the necessary tools."

Reflections

Some Possible Ways of Explaining How, and How Well, and Why the Metaphor Works—and, Therefore, Somewhat Indirectly but Quite Operationally Revealing Its Metaphor-ness

- (a) to strongly get across the pervasive nature and regularity of the systematic listening taking place when the person "was overheard," ordinary listening and mere eavesdropping are amplified to the infamous program of governmental spying associated with the fictional political figure of "Big Brother" in British author George Orwell's novel 1984; this quite large sibling (a "brother" who is "big") is not actually anyone's brother or even second-cousin-once-removed but he (He) is metaphorically called "brother" to emphasize the almost familial aspect of the surveillance—just like (or just enough like) the kind of concerned eavesdropping a member of your very own family would do. Note that my use of "just like" (the "just" being purposefully added to emphasize the "like") helps to get at the essence of how a metaphor does its thing, how it operates, how it works—and why it is uncommonly effective when done well;

- (b) to scatologically communicate just how scared a person might be in a particularly frightening situation, the image is created through the diction choice of "not-in-good-company" language of someone so petrified (my use of "petrified" is also a metaphor) that he or she might lose it, as tortured prisoners have been known to lose control of their bowels. In this bathroom metaphor, as in all metaphors, the words are never to be taken *literally* (actually meaning what they would appear to say). Metaphors are imaginative *configurations* of language; they are examples of *figurative* (non-literal) phrase-making, which is why you will hear metaphors referred to as examples, in any language, of "figures of speech." (More fundamentally, to my mind, a metaphor is a "figure of thinking" that reveals itself in a person's speech or writing.) A metaphor can be thought of as an imaginative comparison of one real situation or object (which is crying out to be conveyed intensely, or creatively, or dramatically) to another real situation or object that exists in the world but is not physically present at this particular moment in this particular same place;

- (c) to stress "the stress" a person feels when told that he or she uses metaphors all the time and takes this news quite negatively (fear of the unknown and of the-not-well-understood is very, very, very stressful), the stress is imaginatively seen as a medical condition in need of immediate treatment toward a hoped-for cure;

- (d) to effectively get across the full force of the dreaded consequences were a few people to learn of the person's unknowing and, perhaps, unauthorized use of "metaphors all the time," the few people are exaggerated into the entire "world" and the news is visualized, creatively, as wind currents from Mother Nature (another metaphor) as they waft through the air as though they were a deadly virus. Goodness, there we go talking even more metaphorically while trying to explain the metaphor under examination (like a doctor's physical examination—oops, did it again);

- (e) to exaggerate the depth of a person's belief that he or she is not sophisticated enough to talk in metaphors, the well-known intensity of a cult's indoctrination of its members into a fixed belief system is invoked;

- (f) to intentionally choose the word "manage" may well be metaphorically motivated (as well as soundly alliterative) since the *denotational* (strictly dictionary) meaning of "manage" often carries with it the *connotational* (associational) meaning of "bossy," "controlling," "manipulative"—all attributes that sophisticated persons can lay claim to;

- (g) peasant? Who's a "peasant"? No one, actually—and that's the point of this very emphatic comparison. The maker of this metaphor wants the audience for this metaphor to see and hear and feel the well-known image of a peasant; that way, the "mere-ness," the relative smallness, the striking insignificance of the peasant will be conveyed in high contrast to the not-at-all-"mere" sophisticate;

- (h) which particular tools do you see when you picture the peasant? Which "tools" can you visualize in the hands of the sophisticate? Which other kinds of tools (perhaps metaphorical ones) do you think of when you think of the various and sundry "ways" sophisticates have for "managing"?

Reflections

If Your Language Is Driven by Metaphors, When Should You Put Your Foot Down and Apply the Brakes?

Once you realize that you use metaphors all the time (okay, a lot) in your thinking, once you hear in your speaking and recognize in your writing that your language is regularly "driven" by metaphors (and, yes, "driven" as used here is a recognizable metaphor), then when should your personal "radar" (extending the metaphor) let you know that it is time to "apply the brakes" (extending the metaphor further)? By the way, did you notice as you made your way through this paragraph that it's getting easier and easier for you to spot a metaphor? That's partly because of how much *mental visualization* metaphors make use of and partly because of how frequently metaphor-making results in *hyperbole* (intended and obvious exaggeration).

Well, to get back to when to put the brakes on in your making of metaphors, the key (the car's ignition key?, no, that's really overdoing it) is to try to be consciously on the lookout for any tendency on your part (or on mine!) to, well, overdo it. If the purpose of using a metaphor is to get a listener or reader to perk up and really pay attention to what you are saying, if you talk in too many metaphors too often, what you are saying will have the opposite effect: it will sound like noise (the comparison to noise is, of course, a metaphor).

One way to monitor and manage the metaphors you come up with for possible use is to honestly evaluate just how well you are making the intended comparison of one thing to another for the goal of getting your audience to concentrate on that first thing. The first thing is "the" thing; the second thing is only imaginatively there for the purpose of getting across the "very, very" or "really, really" thought you're emphasizing about that first thing.

Now that you're starting to get the hang of the why and how of metaphors, here are some things you should know about other people's metaphors—the metaphors you come upon in your reading and hearing: if you're not sure whether what you're hearing or reading is a metaphor, try turning the comparison you heard or read into a phrase that begins with "just like . . . ." (There are those who will tell you that using only "like" at the start of the phrase is sufficient, but there are times when unnecessary confusions will result; that is much less often the case with the use of "just like" (or "simply like" or "remarkably like"). Comparisons that are *direct* and *concise*—like figuratively thinking of a situation in terms of "Big Brother"—reveal themselves as metaphors when rephrased in your mind less concisely and more indirectly as "just like Big Brother." (Notice how much easier it is to spot, and, thus, understand, the figurative nature of the comparison being made through this bit of rephrasing.)

A word (or two) of warning: not every comparison we think, or speak, or write, or hear, or read is a metaphor. Speakers and writers of English regularly use comparison and contrast in order to *relate two actual things inhabiting the same general space and time to each other for the purpose of directly communicating which is "more whatever" than the other.*

For example, to say that something is larger than something else, or more expensive than something else, is to make a simple comparison, generally by using the common suffix (word ending) "er" on a word as a comparative ending or by using, in front of the word under consideration, the comparative word "more"; in such "ordinary," non-figurative comparisons, two actual things are being looked at together at the same time in order to determine which one of the two is "more" whatever or "er" (more "more"). And let's not forget superlatives (they're the best!); superlatives are ordinary, non-figurative comparisons taken to the extreme; superlatives (note the "super") use the suffix "est" or the superlative word "most" to take a comparison to its "more-est," its "most."

In addition (and remembering my earlier recommendation of the phrase "just like" over just "like"), not every use of the word "like" in English is a lead-in to a metaphor. Clearly, "like" can be the word that means "prefer" (and just this side of "love") when it is encountered in such sentences as "I like you more than I can say" (after which, silence, apparently). There is also the non-standard (and I—like—believe, irritating) use of "like" by some younger speakers of English, like, when they don't, like, know, like, what they are going, like, to say, like, next. What's not to like about that? Everything!

Some people will tell you that there is a special kind of metaphor (with its own special name—the *simile)* involved when you speak in the less direct, less concise way of speaking metaphorically, as in "Our government is like Big Brother" (as distinguished from the more direct, more concise, and harder to recognize metaphor "Our government is Big Brother"). I've never been partial to this distinction (but you should be aware of its existence); it seems, to me, that singling out similes as special has the tendency to gloss over the fact that *all similes are metaphors* at the same time that it downplays the greater creative power—which *is* special—of the harder to coin non-simile version of metaphor.

Singling out similes as special also raises for some people the unnecessary question of whether all metaphors are similes, which, of course, they're not; the only metaphors that are similes are the ones that actually start with words and phrases like "like," "just like" and, get ready for this, "as if" or "as though," as in "She couldn't get over the feeling that her nation's government thought of its citizens as though they were babies in need of a vigilant 'big brother.'"

So, what it comes down to for me (and may for you) is a preference for generally discounting the existence of the simile *as a concept* because of the definitional emphasis I put on the purpose behind the mindful act of thinking in metaphors as opposed to the practical wording of a particular metaphor as its diction choices play out. However, if the greater recognizability of the form of a simile works for you *conceptually*—the acknowledgment of certain cues in the language to the upcoming appearance of a metaphor—then I won't take it personally. In fact, I'll "let sleeping dogs lie." (I really, really won't make a fuss, a stir, a to-do about it.) However, as the Scottish novelist Ali Smith says in her 2013 novel ARTFUL, in a play on the word "smile" in a song the American singer Nat King Cole made famous: "Simile, though your heart is breaking."

But back to "putting the brakes" on metaphors when you're "cooking with gas." Oh, didn't I mention I was cooking with gas? That's what I was doing when I was making excessive use of metaphors. Well, of course I didn't—because I wasn't *actually* "cooking with gas." (For a certain generation of Americans, "cooking with gas" was a favorite metaphor for getting across the idea that you were really, really or very, very into something that you were doing—and that it was going along quite well, thank you.)

That particular "gas" metaphor was, in fact, so common (in the days before electric stoves replaced gas stoves in many parts of the country) that it rather quickly became a cliché—and clichés need to be retired like a computer operator with severe arthritis of the fingers and wrists (simile, anyone?) needs to be retired (with health benefits and a pension). "Cooking with gas" had been used so often for so long that it no longer could attract the necessary metaphorical attention for focusing understanding. It was now tired, trite, and tone-deaf. (It was also a good representative example of how some clichés historically lose their meaning when the reality that sustains them and allows them to make sense changes. Cooking with what? Gas? Huh?)

Most clichéd figures of speech, however, take a long while to disappear because, like old soldiers, they *don't* die, they just fade away (or, to purposely mix the metaphor, they have "a long shelf life"). Because clichés both reflect and reflect on your thinking, good thinkers understand that metaphors that have become clichés need to be recognized for what they are and avoided "like the plague." A relatively new cliché of a metaphor that sees the United States as "a salad bowl" of diversity has begun to replace the older clichéd metaphor that sees the country as "a melting pot" of assimilation; your preference may depend on your sense of history and on your politics.

Finally, as you work to clamp down on clichés and make a mindful effort to create your own original metaphors, be careful not to "mix your metaphors." Good thinkers whose language is English tend look down on the practice of adding one metaphor onto another when the addition produces a mix that doesn't match; however, extended metaphors that work are effective because the original metaphor is consistently built on, not simply added to, and the match appears organic. With mixed metaphors, it's "all apples and oranges," so to speak metaphorically. Really egregious mixed metaphors stand out like a sore thumb in a field where it's raining cats and dogs.

Truth be told, those of us who are working to think, speak, and write in meaning-conveying metaphors will, from time to time, in the gush of exuberance, come up (and out) with two or more fresh metaphors from different worlds (worlds that don't seem to mix naturally or well). Or, we will make use of metaphors we selectively lift from other people that are not only clichés but clichés that don't normally travel in the same circles. Forgive us, for we—sometimes—know what we are doing.

And Likewise, by Analogy

And now for some almost last words (or pairs of words): metaphors (and, therefore, also similes) sometimes present themselves as ordered pairs (analogies)—so already you can confidently conclude that analogies are fundamentally about association, resemblance, and correspondence. It is probably most helpful to think of analogies as utterances of pairings that single out one particular aspect in a relationship of specific items that is essentially or dramatically similar to a comparable aspect in a second relationship.

For many American college-bound high school students, analogies are also a famous feature of the College Board's Scholastic Aptitude Test (SAT), which—through its use of analogy problems ("A is to B as C is to *what?*")—tests both logical thinking and vocabulary development. In these verbally posed SAT analogies, one pair of words is presented as similar to an incomplete but implied other pair. The intellectual task for the test-taker is to consider the various ways in which the two pairs are similar and narrow them down to one "best" likeness.

So, for example, an SAT paired-words analogy question with its familiar colon punctuation marks might posit that hand : palm :: foot : ??? In one's mind (or aloud) this gets read as "hand" is to (is related to) "palm" as "foot" is to (is related to) "what other specific thing?" The sought-for answer is "sole" and the thinking behind that answer is that while there are certainly a number of different ways in which something as specific as one's hand is meaningfully related to that hand's palm, *only* the skin surface aspect of that connection *also* figures predominantly in the relationship of one's foot to the sole of that foot.

The good news for critical thinkers is that SAT-type analogy problems require problem solving—and commercially prepared worksheets filled with them can be mentally stimulating; the less good news is that their "colon-ized" format can also be, for some, an unnecessary part of the problem. However, spoken and written analogies in our everyday personal and professional communications can sound and look a lot less puzzling to someone who is listening or reading carefully, but even they can be problematic, oversimplifying a similarity or selecting to highlight a perhaps less relevant relationship.

For instance, thinking out loud analogously, I might say that the good thinker, like the hated (and wary) monarch who has his soup first sipped by a servant, shouldn't swallow an argument by analogy without chewing on it first. (I think this is also a good example of an analogy that makes an okay initial impression but doesn't quite hold up when fully digested. *What do you think?*) Let the buyer beware: particularly in flights of rhetoric and logic, arguments using analogies are sometimes intentionally crafted to strengthen political and philosophical opinions even when the sense behind the similarity is weak or non-existent.

Nevertheless, making use of aptly chosen analogous situations has proved effective in such explain-and-convince fields as morality, law, linguistics, science, engineering, and business. Here's why: by invoking analogous situations, communicators are, in effect, mining a kind of anticipated empathy since what they are basically saying is: "You know how *you* think and feel about such-and-such? Well, that's just how *I* think and feel about *my* such-and such."

Here's one such passionate feeling from a September 2013 opinion piece on "How to Fall in Love With Math" in "The New York Times" by Manil Suri, a mathematics professor at the University of Maryland:

> Each time I hear someone say, "Do the math," I grit my teeth . . .; so many people identify mathematics with just one element: arithmetic. Imagine, if you will, using "Do the lit," as an exhortation to spell correctly. As a mathematician, I can attest that my field is really about ideas above anything else.

By counting on the obvious-to-many-of-us diminishment of the beauty of literature to little more than the convenience of correct spelling, Professor Suri uses empathy to get across an understanding of a mathematics lover's annoyance at the glibness (even when unintentional) inherent in the words "Do the math."

Mind Set

In Conclusion

Enough said, for now, about the everyday pervasiveness in our thinking (and speaking and writing) about that figure of speech the Greeks called "metaphor" (the Greek word was itself a metaphor that meant to "transfer" or "carry across")—the idea behind the coinage being that metaphors "carry" meaning from one word, or image, or idea to another in order to suggest a similarity. However, if you want to immerse yourself in a figurative "host" of metaphors ("host" being a metaphor for, well, you can make a list of what you think it is a metaphor for), any online search under the more literal "lists of metaphors" will get you there swiftly and directly.

Assessing Your Thinking

www

So where does this leave us on our "journey" to the realization that so much of the good thinking (and too much of the muddled thinking) human beings do is, metaphorically speaking, speaking in metaphors? Do you think you've nailed it, metaphorically speaking? And if you've seen the metaphor of hitting the nail on the head as a metaphor for finally understanding something you were having trouble achieving (along with some of the other metaphors "hidden" in the content of this chapter), then you may have already realized that the very name of the "worldwide web" (www) is itself a metaphor; to see that really clearly (the opposite of the metaphor "as clear as mud"), just mentally visualize a spider web and then zero in on how an imaginative comparison is being made to the similarities that focus your thinking on what is essential about going online.

And speaking of the computer's "www" as a metaphor, a review in "The New York Times" of the 2013 novel TAIPEI by Tao Lin makes a point of noting that "almost all of this novel's metaphors and similes emerge from the author's experience of the Internet and his sense of the way it is colonizing consciousness." The reviewer then gives the following examples of how this is true of the novel's main character, Paul—and since we're now in an Assessing Your Thinking section of **Good Thinking**, you will want to explain the "how" of these metaphors (and of this extend metaphor) to your own satisfaction:

> Paul thinks of "the backs of his eyelids as computer screens." When he wakes in the morning, he feels his memories downloading into his mind, like PDF files. A social interaction makes him feel "a sensation not unlike clicking 'send' for a finished draft of a long e-mail."

Assessing Your Thinking

"All the World's a Stage"

But let's, like so many mentioners of metaphors over the past four hundred years, give William Shakespeare, the bard of Stratford-upon-Avon, the last word on this subject. In those lists of metaphors you can find online, one of the metaphors you will surely come upon is the justifiably famous one in which Shakespeare sees the world we live in as so very similar, in several key ways, to the theatrical stage upon which the thirty-seven plays he wrote were performed (you might want to try your hand at continuing the metaphor with related similarities, thus producing your own "extended metaphor"). Here is how Shakespeare begins:

> All the world's a stage, and all the men and women merely players. They have their exits and their entrances . . . .

11

Thinking Wittily (A Walk on the Wilde Side)

Think About It

In this chapter you will discover:

- why "wit" is even in a book about thinking,
- why they're wild about Wilde,
- how to channel Oscar Wilde.

Mind Set

To wit: would we have words in the English language like "nitwit" and "half-wit" if being "witty" wasn't a kind of thinking? Think about it.

What Do You Think?

Well, if you thought about it, what *do* you think? And why?

Reflections

The Humor Or Not of Wit

So, to get at an understanding of what being a wit is like and how it actually involves a kind of thinking, let's bypass a standard dictionary definition and, instead, begin with an attempt at an explanation of the difference between what we call "wit" and what we consider a "sense of humor." It seems to me that humor arises out of character and situation and is, for the person in the situation, more of a way of the heart than a way of the mind; humor is an attempt to deal with and survive the possibly serious in a way that doesn't take it all that seriously. As a result, humor is a "way" of life.

Wit, on the other hand, arises more out of studied "reflection," an after-thought of the analytical mind; wit looks back in its thoughtful ease on a situation that someone has experienced and lived to tell about; or, wit looks reflectively at a universal condition and has a smart remark to make about it from the safe distance of another time and other place.

In intention, wit, unlike humor, can be mean-spirited and hurtful (up there with sarcasm): the joke can be on us. Wit is paradoxical: it is often simultaneously thoughtful and thoughtless, particularly when its target is less the human condition and more a specific human being. While humor can be employed both sympathetically and empathetically, wit comes across more often as above-the-fray intellectual commentary on either the "person-ality" *in* a situation or the universality *of* a situation. People who are "wits" tend to pronounce rather than converse—and because humor has more heart and is, therefore, more "warm" while wit exudes the cool-ness of the mind, it is no accident that the word "wit" is often linguistically married to "wisdom," as in the wit and wisdom of (your favorite wit's name here).

To get a more specific sense of what I mean by this, you can do no better than to channel "the wit and wisdom" of the Irish writer Oscar Wilde (who wittily said of himself: "I have nothing to declare but my genius"). Wilde's sentences (in at least two senses of that word) are often "one-liners," like the unexpected, unpredicted, incongruous yet somehow mindfully inevitable, about-faced punchline to a joke, where you abruptly get the point of the joke without most of the joke's "plot" being provided; literally scores of examples of Wilde's witticisms can be found in online lists compiled from his dramatic and other writings (and even from his deathbed!—I make use of a "final" quote from Wilde near the end of Chapter 1 of this book).

Wilde's way with words is the stuff, literally, of legends (as a convicted prisoner waiting to be taken to one of Queen Victoria's jails, Wilde quipped: "If this is how Queen Victoria treats her prisoners, then she doesn't deserve to have any"). If you read enough of Wild's repartee in a row (I provide an assortment of thirty below), you will get both their feel and flavor, what they mostly have in common, and some insight into why they work so well; you will even figure out how to sound like Oscar Wilde himself if you think you might like to try your mind and your hand at a witty commentary or a verbal "take" on anything the world offers up to you for your considered opinion. It's possible you could develop into a wit. Be careful, though: this is something you should practice only at home—and it is definitely not something you will want to take on lightly and only partly succeed in—then you would be a half-wit.

What Do You Think?

Wilde's Witty Way With Words: An Assortment of 30— Because Who Can Trust a Witticism Over 30?

- I always pass on good advice. It is the only thing to do with it. It is never of any use to oneself,
- Arguments are to be avoided: they are always vulgar and often convincing,
- All women become like their mothers. That is their tragedy. No man does. That's his,
- Bigamy is having one wife too many. Monogamy is the same,
- An idea that is not dangerous is unworthy of being called an idea at all,
- Men marry because they are tired; women, because they are curious; both are disappointed,
- A little sincerity is a dangerous thing, and a great deal of it is absolutely fatal,
- Experience is simply the name we give our mistakes,
- A true friend stabs you in the front,
- Always forgive your enemies—nothing annoys them so much,
- I am not young enough to know everything,
- Children begin by loving their parents; after a time they judge them; rarely, if ever, do they forgive them,
- I have the simplest of tastes. I am always satisfied with the best,
- A thing is not necessarily true because a man dies for it,
- There is only one thing in life worse than being talked about, and that is not being talked about,
- It's not whether you win or lose, it's how you place the blame,

- The old believe everything, the middle-aged suspect everything, the young know everything,
- There is no sin except stupidity,
- He hadn't a single redeeming vice,
- It is only the modern that ever becomes old-fashioned,
- A pessimist is one who, when he has a choice of two evils, chooses both,
- I never travel without my diary; one should always have something sensational to read in the train,
- Selfishness is not living as one wishes to live, it is asking others to live as one wishes to live,
- When the gods wish to punish us, they answer our prayers,
- One can always be kind to people about whom one cares nothing,
- To get back my youth I would do anything in the world, except take exercise, get up early or be respectable,
- Life is far too important to be taken seriously,
- I am so clever that sometimes I don't understand a single word of what I am saying,
- One's real life is often the life that one does not lead,
- Whenever people agree with me I always feel I must be wrong.

Assessing Your Thinking

If you feel you've got the hang of it, respond in your personal journal to as many of the following questions as you choose:

- where did you find that wit shares with joke-telling a punch at the end that is unexpected but, once you see how often that mechanism is employed, you learn to generally expect the unexpected and specifically try to make educated guesses or predications as to what it might consist of?

- can you explain why there were particular examples of Wilde's use of wit where you "saw it coming"?
- once you discovered that there were certain universal subjects that Wilde particularly liked to quip about, why was it easier for you to accurately predict how a witticism would end (you "just knew it") when you realized at the start of the witticism that Wilde was at that particular content again?
- how much lateral thinking did you find yourself using once you discovered that it was an effective way into the nature of wit? Why do you suppose this is so?
- do you think you could "backwards predict" the "plot" opening of a Wilde witticism if you were given its "punchline" of a clincher? Test this out with several of the thirty quips presented in the assortment,
- write a few of your own Wilde witticisms—use a representative or universal subject or content and choose your wording to reflect Wilde's inimitable (literally, "can't be matched or imitated") style, which you are, paradoxically, being now asked to imitate; be "cool" in your wisdom.

Mind Set

In Conclusion

Since Oscar Wilde absolutely must have the last word in a chapter on his way of thinking ("thinking well" as distinct from "good thinking"), what follows is one of the most famous of Wilde's "quotations" from his wonderfully witty and wise play "The Importance of Being Earnest" (which you should go read, or re-read, or see a production of as soon as is humanly possible): "To lose one parent, Mr. Worthing, may be regarded as a misfortune; to lose both looks like carelessness."

12

Thinking Symbolically (It's Way More Representative of Your Thinking Than You Think)

Think About It

In this chapter you will discover:

- how, and when, and why a symbol "stands for" something else (when it is not sitting down on the job),
- how to knock the legs out from under a symbol that may still stand for something but has been standing for that same something for so long that the symbolism is little more than a crutch that, in effect, undermines good thinking.

Mind Set

"Critical" as in "Analytical" Or "Critical" as in "That Stinks!"?

Many, many years ago I saw a short (five-minute-or-so) film that has stayed long in my memory. Call it "memorable"; actually, it was called "The Critic," and it consisted solely of two things:

a colorful abstract design that remained the only thing on the screen for the film's entire running time; and the increasingly more frustrated (nay, more exasperated) off-screen vocal commentary of an older man as he thought out loud about the meaning of what he (and we, the audience for the film) were being made to look at for a full five minutes. (The film would have felt much longer if the sound track had not been so hilarious.)

As the old man (whom we never see but whose recognizable voice was that of the classic comic writer and comic actor Mel Brooks) struggled to make some sense of what might well have been categorized as an abstract work of "art," his scripted words with their distinctive tone of voice juxtaposed against ("placed alongside of"—or in this case, "over") the film's single visual image, created the complex humor of an otherwise very simple film.

Not so incidentally, *juxtaposition* is a powerful thinking technique: putting two things (words, phrases, images) near or next to each other can generate a totally new moment of meaning (think of juxtaposing as the bringing of a lighted match alongside, well, you name it, as long as there is the potential for "Fire!"). You'll readily notice juxtaposition being used effectively on you by others (in your reading, in your listening), and you'll probably want to incorporate it into your own communication "bag of tricks" (metaphorically speaking).

What happens with all effective use of juxtaposition, as happens in the film "The Critic," is the production of a new meaning, or idea, or point of view that is more than just the mathematical addition of two separate and distinct meanings; instead, juxtaposition is like two separate "elements" from a kind of Periodic Table of Elements reacting chemically with each other to create something entirely new and different from its component parts. A veritable explosion of meaning!

In the film "The Critic," its five minutes of screen time go by in "real time," which is to say that the five minutes we spend watching the film is the exactly the same amount of time the increasingly cranky old man spends viewing and commenting on the piece of abstract "art." (In case you were wondering—a good thing for thinkers to be in the habit of—there are actually a few long-ish modern stage plays that play out in real time: for one example, the 90-minute play *"'night, Mother"* (1983) by the American writer Marsha Norman, has a clock on the kitchen wall of the set that shows ninety minutes in the lives of the play's two characters (a daughter contemplating suicide and her mother whom she is telling her plans to) go by as the audience watches the intermission-less play.)

As audience for "The Critic," we spatially and temporally come to share the old man's sense of failure at coming up with "the right answer" to the question "what is the meaning of the abstract design?" As we eavesdrop on the man's "critical" (analytical) comments as well as on his "critical" (evaluative) comments about the depicted work of art, we increasingly empathize with his frustration. Finally, in utter defeat, the old man proclaims with great certainty as the film's five minutes come to an end: "It must be some symbolism thing"—and, then, after a meaningful pause, "It must be symbolic of JUNK."

What Do You Think?

- what experiences like this one of the increasingly frustrated old man have you had with something whose "hidden" symbolic meaning (or absence of meaning) caused you to be puzzled, confused, frustrated, annoyed, and, perhaps, defeated?

- did you finally conclude that the fault was yours (*you* "failed") and give up your quest to find some sense in something symbolic or, like the "critic" in "The Critic," did you ultimately conclude that you were being put upon—that there was no real meaning to be found because your "leg was being pulled," metaphorically speaking (that this "thing" was nothing more than "junk" posing as significantly meaningful "art")?

- do you think the old man actually succeeded in making sense of the abstract design—*that he got his mind to go from "Huh?" to "Hmm" to "Aha!"*? If so, what sense did he make of it, and why have you come to that analytical conclusion?

- "The Critic" has stayed in this writer's memory for decades; what thoughts do you have as to why that might be so?

- when asked what his abstract film was all *about*, one filmmaker answered: "It's about five minutes long." What do you think of this reply as a response to the hunger for meaning on the part of an audience? What do you think of this reply from a filmmaker's (an artist's) perspective? Because . . . ?

- in general, what is your feeling about "all this symbolism stuff"—and why is that?

- the American writer Gertrude Stein once said that "a rose is a rose is a rose"; what do you think she was trying to get across in this famous repetitive remark—and do you agree with the point you think she was making?

Reflections

Symbols as Figures of Speech, as Imaginative Configurations

Although "The Critic" was a very short film and its five minutes depicted an actual five minutes in the life of the narrator, for the old man that baffling experience felt like much more than five minutes. Symbols in art (and music, and literature—and life) can do that to us.

Symbols, like metaphors, result from imaginative ways of thinking (and speaking, and writing) in order to call attention to something considered special in a special, uncommon way. However, the key thing about symbols is that they stand for or represent *both* themselves and that other something *in addition to* themselves. Sometimes they are relatively easy to spot in other people's thinking when we hear them or read them—they both stand for and stand out; sometimes, not so easy: they're there—but are almost invisible until they "hit" you. Sometimes the "motion" someone else's use of symbolism makes is the stirring of an "emotion" in you; other times, other people's use of symbolism can go right over your head.

Also, symbols are so much a part of how we think as human beings that tried and true symbols (originally uncommon but now way too commonplace) come out of our own mouths (or off our own hands, if we're doing some writing) without our being consciously aware. As with clichéd metaphors, symbols that have become clichés were once full of "sound and fury" but now signify nothing all that special.

At this point you may be hoping for some examples of symbols (have I been stalling?), so let's go for one of the most familiar ones, where an actual object is presented for the human experience *both* for itself *and* for something else it is going to stand for or represent. A nation's flag (any nation's flag and "flag" in any language) is as good an example as any and better than most because it is so "out there."

Clearly, a flag is a flag (is a flag?). The old man in "The Critic" would certainly agree that "a flag is a flag"; he can see *that*—there's nothing abstract about it; it's concrete—he can touch any flag he puts his hand to. But a nation's flag, by common agreement among its "patriotic" citizenry, has come to *also* represent—without losing any of its fabric of "flag-ness"—not only highly positive *feelings* about the nation by its citizens but also the nation's wartime *history*, the nation's *struggles and triumphs, the nation itself*. None of the words I've italicized are made of anything as concrete and tangible as "fabric"; yet these abstract ideas (you can't put your hand to them) have been somehow "made" concrete through their identification with a tangible piece of cloth and that tangible piece of cloth's identification with them.

"But it's *just* a flag," the old man "critic" might insist in frustration (just as, if handed a rose, he would probably state emphatically that "a rose is a rose is a rose"); he doesn't get the symbolism; he doesn't "see" it. The old man is telling it like it "is"—as would any others who see nothing beyond the material flag, none of the associations that have accrued to it, none of the flag's symbolic meaning. But to those "into" the symbolism (in the know about the symbolism), that flag is, yes, still a flag but it's also—and, it turns out, much more significantly—all that it represents to that nation's citizenry, all that it stands for, all that it symbolizes.

In fact, hang it at half staff (on land), or half mast (at sea), or not accidentally upside down and you are knowingly trying to communicate to others certain additional meanings—further symbolic sense; display it "inappropriately" by, for example, reconfiguring it actually, not simply imaginatively, and wearing it as an article of clothing (in other words, treating it as nothing more than a piece of cloth to be shaped for a particular practical purpose) and you might have both a symbolic and an actual fight on your hands. (A rose is not a rose is not a rose.)

So symbols are always in the mind of the beholder. Particular symbols work for "us" only when their meaning is shared and "properly" understood; it takes two or more individuals in agreement about whether our "thinking in symbols" is a "common" sense. Otherwise, a thing is what the thing "is"—and that could even be actual, non-symbolic "junk."

Besides objects, symbolism can be found in images, and sounds, and, of course, in words. Language in and of itself is a complete symbolic system: we agree on which of those funny sounds we make with our mouths make sense with particular meanings and which are gibberish or noise; and we agree on which of those funny-looking marks we make with our pens or more expensive letters-of-the-alphabet-making machines that we buy (such "magic-markers" known as computers), accurately represent those funny sounds that make sense and which "representations" are nonsense or, what amounts to pretty much the same thing for "us," a "foreign" language.

Since human beings mostly think through language and in words, if we want to be good thinkers we should have at least a reasonable grasp of how verbal symbolism works when we come upon it in our reading and listening. And we should have a more than okay "grasp" of verbal symbolism if we want to make symbols work for us in getting across our meanings to others through the manipulation of the language that we speak and write.

Assessing Your Thinking

- how do we go about getting that grasp? Well, grabbing a good book (a novel, preferably, because of its, it would seem, natural abundance of symbols) and reading it with relish will expose you to that author's use of verbal symbols to reveal character, advance plot, establish an atmosphere, set a mood, sound a tone, emphasize a theme. The relationship between reading and thinking is circular: the more you read and think about what you're reading (while and after), the better a thinker you'll become; and the better a thinker you are (or have become), the more you will "get" out of your reading as you read—and then afterwards, when you're sure to find yourself thinking about it some more,

- how do the pieces of fabric known as the flag of the United States of America and as the flag of the Confederate States of American differ in size, shape, fabric, color, design, decorative elements, and any other aspect? What symbols do you find in either and both?,

- most of the Union or "northern" states thought of it as and called it "The Civil War." Most of the Confederate or "southern" states thought of it as and called it "The War Between the States." Is there any symbolism to be found in these different ways of "wording" the "same" war? Explain why you think the way you do,

- would you think that there is something symbolic about this particular chapter's being one of the shortest chapters in this book? Talk about why you think the way you do.

Mind Set

In Conclusion

Human beings speak both informationally and figuratively (using metaphors, hyperbole, symbols, and other figures of speech); with our use of spoken and written language (both reflections of our thinking minds), we can both state the facts and "express" our feelings about them.

Sometimes, as for many people with symbolism, the code of the "expression" seems difficult to break. Sometimes, like the frustrated old man in the film "The Critic," we think everyone else has the key except us. Sometimes, we may be right, and, sometimes, everyone else is thinking the same thing.

13

Thinking Ironically (Or At Least "Interestingly")

Think About It

In this chapter you will discover:

- what the three most commonly used kinds of irony are,
- why there is no "iron" in irony (how verbal irony differs from sarcasm),
- why irony is even considered to be "good thinking."

Mind Set

It's ironic that this next-to-last chapter of this self-improvement book on "good thinking" should deal with the kind of thinking, speaking, and writing that is considered "ironic."

No it isn't—and I'm not being ironic. I'm lying, actually.

What Do You Think?

And you're thinking (I'm hoping): why is the author of **Good Thinking** lying? (And superstitiously—which is not "good thinking"—could it have anything to do with the number 13 at the top of this chapter?)

Reflections

Let Me Take You Into My Confidence (Not a Con Game)

Thinking back on the previous chapter on "thinking symbolically," I am struck by the fact that in our mental universe, recognizable symbols are all around us but, interestingly, in our everyday communication with others, we rarely name or label or categorize our symbolic thinking as such; we rarely say something like, "It's symbolic that blah, blah, blah" or "Symbolically, I find that . . . ."

Is this because we actually don't talk that much in symbols of our own creation? Or is that when we actually talk in the "handed-down" symbols of our common heritage, we want that symbol to speak for itself? Could it be that we want any *symbolic communication* that we make use of to become noticeable only to those who on their own can hear and read correctly our use of symbolic language—no cues to their presence allowed?

On the other hand (which is the way good thinkers "speak with their hands"), our speaking and reading worlds are filled with talkers and writers who cue us about the upcoming arrival of *ironic communication* all the time—including even those times when the irony doesn't show up; it's not that the irony "flight" has been canceled; it was never scheduled to "take off" because the irony "pilot" didn't really know how to fly the irony "plane."

As you probably noticed, like most writers I've just used quotation marks to cue or signal written metaphor-making. With both written and spoken irony, however, the cue is blatant: we tell it and spell it straight out like we think it is.

In fact, the irony "cue" has become a quite noticeable way for some people to *introduce* any point they're about to make that they consider "interesting": the first words out of their mouths will be the words "ironically" or "it's ironic that."

Ironically (more about this actual and purposeful use of "ironically" coming up soon, I promise), too many people who use "ironically" or "it's ironic that" by way of introduction to something they're about to exclaim that they consider oh-so interesting, then go on to say something that is not ironic at all! (Note my purposeful use of the exclamation mark.) They would have been more correct if they had said either "It's interesting that . . ." or "interestingly." And, "interestingly," there is at least one website I'm aware of that devotes itself exclusively to having people decide (by voting!) whether a situation or verbalization they've heard or read about is ironic or not! (You can find it easily by doing a search under "irony," and you may be surprised to see that rarely is there 100 percent agreement on whether something is ironic or not.)

However difficult it my be to be certain in your own mind about whether you're looking at or hearing something truly ironic, you will get better at it with practice as long as you practice the following thinking process (and so here's my promised "coming up soon"):

What makes irony "irony" is this: irony deals in what a listener or reader might logically or realistically expect and how that expectation is thwarted; the anticipated doesn't come about—and what actually arrives, in its place, is unlikely to have been thought of and less likely to have been predicted.

Assessing Your Thinking

Comment on why you agree or not that cueing an upcoming irony is basically a way of saying something like each of the following:

- "get ready to have your expectations knocked for a loop, unfulfilled, reversed,"
- "can you believe this (what I'm about to share with you)!"
- "who would have thought (not I, not you)!"
- "it's unbelievable (and yet that's exactly what happened, you've got to believe me)!"
- "surprise (even if you don't like surprises)!"
- !!!

Reflections

It's Easy to Lie and Be Mistaken About Irony (What's Ironical?)

"Wow!" says the listener or reader. "Wow!" says the irony—and it says it with at least one exclamation mark (either present in print or vocally intoned, heard, or "understood").

So, going back to my deliberate lie at the start of this chapter and my opening words that "it's ironic that the next-to-last chapter of this self-improvement book on 'good thinking' should deal with the kind of thinking, speaking, and writing that is considered "ironic," it would seem that I lied when I wrote "it's ironic" because I have yet to show in these pages that followed that my "cue" set up an alert to something unexpected and surprising about making this book's next-to-last chapter about irony instead of about something else good thinkers need to know about.

What Do You Think?

Perhaps you were expecting a chapter on "who-knows-what"? Or, maybe you were, in point of fact, expecting a chapter that would explore "thinking ironically." And yet, when you read my Mind Set opening cue "It is ironic that," those words had a familiar ring to them, didn't they—and you let them glide right by you (that *was* you, wasn't it?). Or was it simply that you were expecting something, shall we say, "interesting"?

Reflections

It's Not Ironic That There Are At Least Three Major Kinds of Irony

Before we talk any more about irony—actually, about this kind of irony (oh, boy! Is there more than one kind?—and, yes, interestingly, but *not* ironically, there is), we need to first spend just a little bit of time on the two (2!) other kinds of irony. (The even better news is that these two kinds of irony are really not too difficult to explain and understand.)

So, to start, there is dramatic irony. The "dramatic" part comes from the fact that this kind of irony is only present in situations in which an audience is involved with a play, or a movie, or a drama on television and the script has a tense moment coming up. (It wouldn't hurt for you to think of the particular drama known as the horror movie in order to feel the kind of tension that's almost needed. Or maybe it would hurt.) Now, in the script, the story line, the plot line, something bad is about to *happen to* one of the characters or to *be done to* that character by another character. As a member of the audience you are absolutely convinced of this impending doom (thanks to your involvement with the story so far). You know it, the rest of the audience knows it, but what good does that do any of the characters in the drama? They don't know what is to befall them—and they have no clue!

What do you wish you could do with your knowledge? Probably, you want—badly—to somehow share it with the fictional character. But that's the problem. That person is fictional and you're not. (It doesn't matter that the fictional character is being played by a live actor in a live performance on a theater stage.) Your knowledge does that character absolutely no good because you can't (well, you shouldn't) leave your seat, break through "the fourth wall" of theatrical convention, and run up on the stage and rescue the character and save the situation.

But, of course, that's exactly what you want to do, that you wish you could do. And because you can't (and won't), the tension is intense (it's "dramatic" up there on the stage and between the stage and audience). And the irony? Well, the irony exists in the disparity, the gap, the disconnect between what the audience member knows and can do nothing about and what the fictional character doesn't know and can't learn in order for things to "play out" differently from what it says in the script. "How ironic!" we say in these moments of dramatic irony. "If only!"

Next, there is irony of situation. We're not in a theater or in front of a television set. We're in the real world in an actual situation but what we expected that situation to have going for it, what we anticipated about it is missing; instead, in its place, we get something—it's pretty "unsafe to say"—completely unexpected—and it is in that unexpectedness that the disparity, the gap, the incongruity, the disconnect exists.

Mind Set

An Appointment in Samarra

Here's a literary example of irony of situation that has been told in a variety of forms over the years; you may, in fact, be familiar with one or more of the versions of what is most often called the story of an "Appointment in Samarra."

The situation is simple—and basic: a person gets the overwhelming feeling that he is going to die—and soon. Death—usually personified as male (but the British writer W. Somerset Maugham penned a female Death in his 1933 version), usually well on in years, and noticeably stooped over (perhaps from the weight of a customary over-the-shoulder scythe)—is coming to "get him." The person's days are numbered and that number is about to come up. "The grim reaper" has "an appointment" to keep (it is, quite naturally, a mutual appointment), and the grim reaper is always on time.

What to do? How to avoid one's destiny? Hide? Run away? Leave home (no forwarding address)? Go where death (Death) can't find you?

That's what this person decides to do: in order for Death to not find him, he leaves his home city and travels a very far distance to—where?—Samarra (to use the name of an ancient city of note, but it doesn't matter what the name of his secret destination is). And who does the man meet in Samarra, as though by appointment? Death (his death, the death that has his name on it). And why is that? Because, it isn't easy—no, more definitive than that—it is impossible, if you are a believer in fate, to escape death when your time has come; it's the time that's critical, not the place—the place is incidental to the time.

And so, when the man meets Death personified in Samarra and asks him what he is doing there (because the man expected Death to be looking for him all over town in the place he has fled from), Death knowingly responds with something like these "immortal" words: "I'm here to keep my meeting with you. Didn't you realize that we had an appointment in Samarra?"

What Do You Think?

How ironic! And why's that? (Before you read any further.)

Reflections

Life's Little Ironies

Because unexpectedly, for the man caught in the irony of this situation, the very place the man fled to in order to escape death is the very place where death always planned to meet him—and take him. If you appreciate the disparity, the gap, the disconnect between the man's choosing Samarra as a place of refuge and the reality of its being the (fated) place where Death awaits his arrival, then you can appreciate the irony involved, the irony of this situation. Wow! How ironic! What the man needed to know he couldn't possibly have known. Such is life. And such is life filled with these kinds of ironies.

Mind Set

Finally, Verbal Irony

Which brings us to the third major kind of irony: verbal irony. Here, too, the word or words next to the word "irony" in the name of the irony are the key to the particular kind of irony involved;

in verbal irony, the word "verbal" ("verbal" means "using words") alerts us to the fact that any irony to be found will be found not in a scripted drama, and not in a real-life-type situation, but in a person's use of words.

See how easy this is?

Wait, I'm being ironic with my meaning and my choice of words. I don't for a minute believe that "verbal irony" is easy. (Didn't I give you an implied heads-up to that effect a few pages ago, purposely first dealing with dramatic irony and irony of situation (also sometimes referred to as "situational irony") and delaying an analysis of verbal irony because verbal irony is the hardest of the three to put your finger on?)

In verbal irony, your intended meaning (most often in a conversation with another person) is intentionally hidden by a choice of words that—ready for this?—*literally says pretty much the opposite of what you mean; the words selected contradict the meaning intended.*

What I said just a little bit earlier about verbal irony ("See how easy this is?") is *not at all* what I meant; what I really meant was more like: "Wow, verbal irony can be difficult to detect and understand" and "I hope you can pick up by my tone of voice (a tone that might be too subtle for some people who don't spend much time around verbal irony and aren't on the best of terms with it) that my *actual meaning is in my tone*, not in my choice of words. Hope that helps!"

What Do You Think?

Why, then, have I chosen verbal irony to get my meaning across? Why didn't I just say directly that verbal irony is not the easiest thing in the world for the uninitiated to understand, let alone to appreciate? Why am I being so roundabout, possibly ambiguous, and potentially confusing by hiding what I mean (you don't say!) and by saying the opposite of what I actually mean? Well?

Reflections

Why, indeed?

Questions like these almost answer themselves since the very wording of them hints at the fact that sometimes being direct can come across as too strong, or too hurtful, too "too." Verbal irony presents a softer alternative to those who can use it carefully and well (thoughtfully and artfully) and know their audience. With the wrong audience, the irony of the words will be missed (and, thus, the meaning intended will be missed)—and, of course, the meaning communicated will be totally wrong because your words will be saying the very opposite of the meaning you intended. Not only will you not make sense but you may, in fact, find that the very softness of your indirectness comes across as harder than the purposely avoided hardness of directness. How's that for miscommunication!

And, sometimes, the very softness of verbal irony can itself be manipulated by good thinkers (but less nice individuals) and knowingly come across as sarcasm. Most people are familiar with what sarcasm does, how it works, and why it's intended to do what it does. I think of sarcasm as the "evil twin" of verbal irony and try hard to guard against being sarcastic around, with and to other people (it's a battle I don't always win). Sarcasm is worse than "not nice"; sarcasm is "mean-spirited"—and if that's the spirit that momentarily moves you, you should metaphorically "bite your tongue" until the moment passes.

Mind Set

In Conclusion

In point of actual fact, our personal and professional worlds can do with a lot less sarcasm. It is neither instructive nor constructive. Saying something in a sarcastic tone of voice can be painfully honest—but it is the pain that is usually felt by the recipient of the sarcasm, and often at the expense of the content of the intended message.

So, if you want to mix in some indirect communication with your direct communication, practice verbal irony. Practice it in the safety and comfort of your home (yes, despite print advertisements and television commercials to the contrary, "do this at home" with yourself as the intended recipient before you go trying it out among your friends; can you take it as well as you can give it?).

Assessing Your Thinking

A different way to think of verbal irony is to define it backwards from your understanding of sarcasm, viewing verbal irony as sarcasm without the mean streak. Consider the following three spoken sentences:

- "you're acting like an idiot,"
- "now that's being really smart,"
- "now that's being really smart."

Perhaps you don't *see* any difference between the last two sentences, and yet you believe that the first sentence is in sharp contrast to the meaning of the other two? Well, how about *hearing any difference*?

In the first sentence, you mean exactly what those five words convey to the person you're talking to. You're being literal and sounding probably borderline annoyed in a statement of what you contend is an irrefutable fact.

In the second sentence, however, the sense is potentially ambiguous: if your tone of voice has been well modulated to get across irony (verbal irony, since you are speaking with words), then you don't at all literally mean what those five words are actually saying; in fact, you mean the opposite of their literal meaning but have purposely chosen words to say the opposite because you know (you hope) that your tone of voice will cue the hearer into realizing that your meaning is actually something like this: "What you are doing right now is somewhat dumb; please stop it because I know you don't want to come across that way."

This use of verbal irony is likely to sound gentler, kinder, more sympathetic than any direct statement of your opinion of the facts ("You're acting like an idiot"). In all likelihood, you can now see why verbal irony can sometimes be completely missed on the printed page (tone of voice, anyone?) and sometimes be mistaken for sarcasm (wrong tone of voice, anyone?). Perhaps this less blunt, safer kind of criticism (of people, of social and political institutions) also explains why verbal irony is often used "to speak truth to power."

In the third sentence, if your tone of voice has been purposely chosen to sound unsympathetic, really annoyed, frustrated, mean, then you are being sarcastic; there is no "iron" in verbal "irony," but there is metaphorical "iron" in sarcasm. As with verbal irony, in sarcasm, you don't at all mean what those five words are saying (you mean—indeed!—the exact opposite of their literal meaning), but you have purposely selected words to say the opposite of that because you hope that your "nasty" tone of voice will cue the hearer that your meaning is actually: "What are you doing? How dumb can you be? I've lost all my patience with you!" (In print, sarcasm would probably have at least one exclamation mark. It's telling.)

So here are some of your communication choices to reflect how your mind is thinking and your heart is feeling:

- say it like it is,
- or say it with verbal irony in order to get across your point indirectly and with no harm intended because, in actual fact, you are purposely avoiding direct communication because you worry that the recipient "can't take it,"
- or say it with sarcasm; caution, you may be asking for trouble (or, in fact, you're intentionally asking for trouble because your act of communication is as much—or more—about your own annoyed feelings and exasperated attitude as it is about the actions you disapprove of that have been committed by the other person).

Assessing Your Thinking

Human Being, I'd Like You to Meet Ms. Death

Think about "cause and effect" and situational irony in connection with W. Somerset Maugham's outside-the-box decision to make Death female in his 1933 version of "Appointment in Samarra."

Consider, in your personal journal, any impact this creative change has for you (in the context of Maugham's specific Bagdad details) on both the ironic and "interesting" meanings of the story: a female-appearing "Ms. Death" (not apparently a "Mr. Death") "jostles" in the great medieval Bagdad marketplace (where he has been sent to purchase provisions for his master) the male servant of a wealthy Bagdad merchant; the "jostling" and a certain "look" on Death's face cause the servant to return home and ask his master for the "loan" of a horse so that he can immediately flee Death by riding to the town of Samarra.

Assessing Your Thinking

The Daily Show of Irony

Watch "The Daily Show with Jon Stewart" on the Comedy Central cable network for a few days in a row, looking for and listening to that program's incidents (situational) and issuances (verbal) of irony. In your personal journal, choose a few of your favorites of each kind to comment on and, yes, explain. As you think about this thinking that you're doing (it'll happen as you write), note whether and why you are starting to change your mind about any example that first struck you as ironic but now seems not so—just wonderfully "interesting."

Assessing Your Thinking

Was That Ironic Or What? Let's Vote on It!

Check out a popular website devoted to having lots of people just like you vote on whether something is ironic or not. Think about their thinking on a whole slew of examples—and think about your thinking about their thinking; finally, cast your vote and explain your thoughtful decision to yourself.

14

Thinking It Through to the End Without Jumping to Conclusions

Think About It

In this concluding chapter you will discover:

- Huh?
- Hmm.
- Aha!

Mind Set

Final thoughts: as an approach for self-improvement, mind your mind.

Reflections

Because, as we are repeatedly, and rightly, being reminded by our world: "A mind is a terrible thing to waste." Anyone's mind—but particularly yours. Now that's memorable.

And here's something else that's memorable: it's always a good time to do some good thinking.

Assessing Your Thinking

How about now?

Mind Set

In Conclusion

And then. And now and then.

And now and again.

And then, again.

CPSIA information can be obtained at www.ICGtesting.com
Printed in the USA
LVOW08s1335080614

389109LV00005B/396/P